being lolita

being lolita

a memoir

alisson wood

FLATIRON
BOOKS
NEW YORK

BEING LOLITA. Copyright © 2020 by Alisson Wood. All rights reserved. Printed in the United States of America. For information, address Flatiron Books, 120 Broadway, New York, NY 10271.

www.flatironbooks.com

Designed by Devan Norman

Library of Congress Cataloging-in-Publication Data

Names: Wood, Alisson, author.
Title: Being Lolita : a memoir / Alisson Wood.
Description: First edition. | New York : Flatiron Books, 2020.
Identifiers: LCCN 2020011918 | ISBN 9781250217219 (hardcover) |
    ISBN 9781250217226 (ebook)
Subjects: LCSH: Wood, Alisson. | Sexually abused teenagers—
    United States—Biography. | High school girls—Abuse of—
    United States. | Teacher-student relationships—United States. |
    Sexual harassment in education—United States.
Classification: LCC HV6592 .W66 2020 | DDC 362.88 [B]—dc23
LC record available at https://lccn.loc.gov/2020011918

Our books may be purchased in bulk for promotional, educational, or business use. Please contact your local bookseller or the Macmillan Corporate and Premium Sales Department at 1-800-221-7945, extension 5442, or by email at MacmillanSpecialMarkets@macmillan.com.

First Edition: 2020

10 9 8 7 6 5 4 3 2 1

To my grandmother,
who would be so scandalized,
and so proud;

to my mother,
who says she will never read this;

and to seventeen-year-old Alisson,
who needed this book most of all.

A word after a word
after a word is power

—margaret
atwood

being lolita

The first time he kissed me, it wasn't on the mouth. I hadn't read the book yet. He told me it was a beautiful story about love.

We would meet in the next town over, a diner off the highway, open all night. I would know what time to meet him in our booth in the back corner because, in the middle of his class, in front of everyone, he would look at me, look into my eyes, and write a number on the blackboard—8 or 9 or 10—and then wipe it away with his other hand. He was an English teacher in my high school. His shirtsleeves were always chalk kissed with white. He was twenty-six. The first time he saw me, I was seventeen.

I would tell my parents I was going to a friend's house or studying somewhere. But, really, I would be sitting across from him for hours, the pastel painting depicting Greek ruins on the wall above him, while he would grade his students' essays and I would sometimes do my Latin conjugations.

Mostly I would write to him, in front of him, and he would bring it home or sometimes read it there under the twenty-four-hour fluorescents and then write back—all over napkins, the paper place mats, scraps from school. We probably covered hundreds of pieces with cursive, but I have only the handful that I hid from him, kept close and stolen away. Before we would leave he'd take the papers and napkins and rip them up, put them into our water glasses, and I would watch them lose their shape and the ink bleed. I wasn't allowed to keep things. I wasn't supposed to call him "Mr." when we were alone, only his first name. But I could never call him that in school. No phone calls, no emails, no touching. He made the rules.

The rules were broken at that diner, in our booth. It was May, summer was almost there, and graduation hung in every classroom, crepe paper and glue-glitter banners filling the halls. A countdown everywhere. You couldn't escape it.

He was trying to teach me about great literature, to prepare me for what I would face as a freshman in college just a few months in the future.

"You should definitely be an English major," he told me, leaning back into the booth, his arms stretched out on top of the bench, taking up so much space across from me. It was the pose that if we were on a date, unseen in a dark theater, would be the transition movement before he put his arm around me. He wouldn't bother with a fake cough, he'd just go for it. I was sure.

He would read me the greats at our table of beige Formica and dull silver: Poe, Dickens, Hawthorne, Carroll. He'd get into it, doing voices when he read *Alice's Adventures in Wonderland*, laughing at literary jokes that I was surely supposed to understand, so I laughed too. I lapped it up, knowing how lucky I was to have this kind of private instruction.

That night he was reading *Lolita* to me, from the beginning of things. He spoke to me in Nabokov's opening lines, languidly: *light of my life, fire of my loins*. I thought it was the most romantic thing ever. But I was ruining it—I had a bug bite and I kept pushing my ankles together, trying to quell the tinge of itch. A child who couldn't sit still.

He began rubbing the edges of the pages with his thumb, harder and harder as his voice grew louder, creating tiny rips in the paper as he stroked them.

Finally, he asked, "A mosquito bite?"

"Yes," I said, an invisible ruler against my spine.

"Don't you have any calamine lotion?"

"Not on me," I said.

"You know," he said, "saliva can stop the itch."

He looked at me. He had green eyes. My flip-flopped feet were on the cracked red leather next to him on the booth, my legs under the table bridging the gap between our benches. Not touching, just beside him. I followed the rules.

He leaned down to my foot next to him and put his lips on my pink, swollen ankle. I felt his breath on my skin.

And it was like every locker in the halls of my high school swung open at once, metal kissing cinder-block walls. It felt just like that.

part i

nymph

1

"I thought she *died*," someone whispered. I didn't know who said it, but I knew they meant me.

I remember the halls of my high school the first day of my senior year. I remember lockers that were green like the flu and taupe, a feeling of illness.

I heard she was committed to a mental hospital, that's where she was last year. Have you seen the scars on her arms?

I remember I woke up early that morning, startled that the day had arrived, changing my clothes over and over. My mother tried to braid my hair, but it wasn't perfect so I took it out.

She flunked out.

I remember I didn't realize I hadn't brushed my teeth until after I was already in the main office, getting my locker combination.

She's such a slut.

I remember walking alone.

There is a long history of loneliness in literature. Of loneliness as a prerequisite to love. Almost like you can't really love someone unless you've been alone and loveless for a long time. At least, if you're a woman. Almost as if this protracted alone time is a purification, prepares a girl to be worthy of a man's love. Think of the Greek myths, the *Odyssey*—Calypso dancing sorcery alone on her island, Penelope waiting twenty years for her wandering husband to return. Think of our fairy tales, the stories we tell our daughters before we put them into bed: of Cinderella toiling in the dust before she can be fitted for those slippers, of Rapunzel living in a tower with only her long hair as silent company. And then her prince comes to rescue her.

Nabokov said that all good stories are fairy tales. At seventeen, I was primed to be someone's princess.

2

It started on purpose. Mid-September: I was taking a creative writing class alongside English, theater, studio art, social studies, math, and Latin. I hated algebra, I loved Latin. I loved writing most of all. My creative writing teacher, Ms. Croix, was new. She didn't know anything about me, only vague notes from the school social worker. In class, she gave me blank pages to fill however I wanted.

She wrote comments with purple ink in my black-and-white mottled composition book, things like "Lovely image!" or "So clear!" or "Wow!" with so many exclamation points. At seventeen, I filled journals like running water.

That Monday, in my notebook at the end of my assignment, in her cursive writing on blue lines, she added, "Come to my room after school today to talk?" The question filled me with fears: *Did she find out about my past? Did she talk to someone? Does she now think I'm crazy too?* I spent the rest of the day with a hollow chest, a stomach of crawling insects.

I opened the door to her classroom certain I was in trouble, that I was again a disappointment to some adult. She wasn't alone. Due to overcrowding, the new teachers had to share their classrooms, and I recognized the man next to her—another new, young English teacher. I must have seen him before in the halls.

Ms. Croix waved me in front of them, the big wooden desk between us. The other teacher was tall with broad shoulders, leaning against the desk. "This is the young woman I was telling you about—this is Alisson," she told him. "Alisson, this is Mr. North."

Right. Him. When you don't talk much, you hear everything—the other girls thought he was *so hot*. His dark hair was long enough to stay behind his ears but still short enough to be appropriate for a grown-up. He had a full shadow of beard, something only a handful of senior guys could manage, and flouted the requirement about teachers wearing ties. I noticed his shirt had a tiny moose embroidered on the side of the pocket—he shopped at Abercrombie & Fitch just like the students did. The mixed signals of adult man and teenage boy in his body radiated through the air, making everything thick and quiet and warm. His eyes fixed on mine and I felt stunned; an animal across a meadow. My breath caught and ribs knit. He was a concoction of the accessible and forbidden, the perfect teenage lollipop.

Mr. North offered his hand. I blinked and breathed and shook his hand strong, like my mother taught me. When our palms pressed against each other, it was like an electric current was made complete, everything suddenly alive in me.

"Hey," he commented, impressed or surprised, or at least pretending to be, by my handshake. My face was still full of questions. Ms. Croix continued to him, "Alisson is a gifted writer, and I thought she could use some extra attention outside of my class." I felt my skin go hot. And then to me, "Mr. North is a writer too—he's agreed to start meeting with you after school."

The teacher started on about his background—Columbia, Cornell—and how we could meet here tomorrow after school, just bring a new journal, just for us. He kept smiling at me. But I kept spinning Ms. Croix's words inside my head—she called me *gifted*. She thought I was good. Good enough to deserve something—Mr. North was a *gift*. I saw myself looking at Mr. North as he looked at me, that slow-motion feeling blooming in my body.

Mr. North put his hand on my shoulder. Would I come see him tomorrow? He wanted to see me. I heard my voice leave my body: *yes*.

3

The thing about princesses is that they're not usually very active in their own lives. Things happen *to* a princess, and all she has to do is say yes. Sometimes she doesn't even have to speak, her prince will just appear, ready for action. He knows what she needs, maybe even more than she does.

Passive princesses abound in fairy tales—they are always falling into danger and the path of some man who has to take the trouble to save them. "Sleeping Beauty" is the most obvious example: a beautiful girl who is trapped in slumber and needs her true love's kiss to awaken. And we cannot forget the Disney classic *Snow White and the Seven Dwarfs*, where yet another princess is saved from the sleep of death by the mouth of her prince.

I had my own troubles with sleep.

My insomnia was sneaky. Sometimes it would happen like this: I would be reading and just keep reading. I would start a new painting, using watercolor and nail polish on canvas

I bought at the crafts store where I worked on the weekends. Or I would have started cutting something out of a magazine, *Seventeen* or *Sassy*, with some specific idea for another collage, and keep cutting and rearranging and smearing purple glue stick and watch it turn clear on the poster board and then I would hear birdsong. Those nights happened by accident. The worst nights, though, I would be in bed the whole time, in the darkness, and just be awake.

My room was small: my twin bed, my grandfather's wooden writing desk, my own phone and answering machine, a bookcase overcome with books. I covered the walls with words and images I cut out. There was a coughing radiator, painted lavender, in the corner. I had an alarm clock that did little. Sometimes my mother would call me after she got to work, around nine or ten in the morning, to see if I was up yet, repeating my name on my answering machine until I picked up the phone: *Ali? . . . Ali? It's your mommy. . . .* A strange song that would infiltrate the last of my dreams. Most days I would wake up to an empty house.

So it was that at the beginning of senior year, I was almost always late to school. The doors automatically locked after the final homeroom bell rang; from then on you had to get buzzed in by the ladies in the front and get a hall pass to go to whatever class you were late to. Most days I was not in homeroom at 7:20 A.M. for my homeroom teacher to mark me as *present*. It took only a few weeks for the women in the office to start rolling their eyes at me when I'd ask for a pen to sign the clipboard, even if I was only a few minutes late. Especially if I walked in closer to lunch.

By this point, it seemed as if everyone had given up on me. I had exhausted my parents' disapproval and emotional investment that had no heartwarming return, and the only thing left was a sort of resignation to my situation. I would get myself to school or I wouldn't. I was seventeen now. It was my problem. It's not like I needed a ride anymore. I had a car that was as old as I was. I had saved the $600 to buy it from cutting fabric at the crafts store and babysitting the previous summer. Gas was only $1 a gallon most weeks, and I was supposed to give my little sister, Lauren, a ride home in the afternoons after her swimming practice. My success or failure was on me.

I had unusual relationships with most of my teachers that year. Other than Ms. Croix and Mr. North, most teachers at Hunt High School didn't think much of me. Notes taken about my instability and excessive absences on formal papers at school; a series of Fs that were part of my permanent record; my legally defined education plan, explaining in detail how I needed special attention and extensions and exceptions—these were all made available to my teachers before I even set foot in their classrooms. It wasn't exactly a glowing introduction. Looking back, I see how these things were meant to help. They weren't intended to make me feel bad about myself. But all they did was make me duck my head as I walked in and out of classrooms, shame seeping out of every pore.

Other students continued to say things in front of me in poorly executed whispers or in notes that were "accidentally" passed to me in class, my name on the folded paper in my hands. A Greek chorus turned cruel.

Do you think she'll show up tomorrow, check yes or no.

She totally ran away last year.

She's such a psycho.

She slept with that guy too???

The rumors were a twisted truth: I had slept with all three of my serious boyfriends in high school. I had been a cutter. I was in a lot of therapists' offices and on a lot of psychiatric medication over the years since middle school. And I had electroconvulsive therapy, ECT, one summer, after a series of months where I would barely leave my room. It wasn't magic, but it had worked. I put on my clothes, walked into the sunshine. I stopped being trapped by sleep. It was enough.

I had run away once, just for the night. I can't remember what fight I had with my parents that spurred my spontaneous flight from home, spending the night driving around in some guy's car. I don't even remember his name. I was sixteen, it was winter; it was too cold to sleep in his car, so we drove and drove, the Smashing Pumpkins album *Mellon Collie and the Infinite Sadness* as our soundtrack in the dark, with only the lights from other cars to see.

And it's true that I physically disappeared from school my junior year. After my rocky first two years, my high school suggested I not bother coming back but instead perhaps consider getting my G.E.D. in night school? My mother not so politely suggested they take a better look at the laws regarding students with disabilities, as by the eighth grade I was already a well-documented depressed, self-mutilating, insomniac adolescent. It was eventually decided that I would attend Pinecrest, a small, therapeutic day school my mother found and forced the school district to pay for.

At the end of my junior year at Pinecrest, my counselor, my homeroom teacher, and the vice principal joined my mother at a large table that seemed to be specifically for meetings like these. I had been in so many of these meetings. The vice principal opened my Pinecrest file—thin, practically roomy—and I had a choice: I could stay at Pinecrest for my senior year and graduate through this program. I had an A in all my classes. I got to take French. There was group therapy every afternoon. I was a model student. Once I saw a boy being restrained by three staff members because he had some sort of psychotic break and started screaming awful things in the hall. Me, I just couldn't figure out why I wasn't happy and couldn't get to school on time. I had mostly stopped cutting myself by then. By Pinecrest standards, I was a success story. My high school diploma would still say Hunt High School, where I was supposed to be, and I was legally protected from disclosing any of my disability accommodations in my college applications. No one would ever have to know.

Or I could go back to Hunt. A chance to be a normal teen girl, everything ordinary and boring. How I longed to be boring. Anything was better than the drama of my depression and mood swings.

"I want to go back to Hunt," I said, a choice that unknowingly led me full speed to the teacher.

I wish I could reach back through space and time and

make a different decision. And then I wonder about things like fate, how sometimes things are just chosen for you, how women are chosen to endure suffering.

Sometimes we are the ones who choose it—Pandora opens the box of suffering herself; even though it is a trap, even though she doesn't understand what is going to happen, it is her own hand that breaks the lock open. How in "The Little Mermaid," the real one, not the Disney fantasy, she chooses to drink the Sea Witch's concoction that will let her dance with legs and the prince instead of just the waves, but every step she takes is like on a sharp knife. In the original story, the whole time the sea nymph is falling in love, her feet are bleeding from supernatural, invisible blades. Even drinking the potion is a sword through her body. And yet it is her choice. She wants this. Every step is hers.

It seems as if no matter how active or passive a girl is, she is still doomed.

Before I returned to Hunt High School and met Mr. North, I had never read Nabokov. I only knew tangentially of the *Lolita* myth—the sexy girl who traps men and so suffers for it. I didn't know that Nabokov was a classicist, that he had published papers and lectured on the intricacies of antiquity and the lessons we should keep. I didn't know how the myths of more than a thousand years ago were indelibly stamped onto his books, how all of this would indelibly stain my life. I didn't know any of this at seventeen. I knew only that I wanted to wake up from these years of sadness and loneliness and be normal. I wanted to go back to my high school.

4

My senior year, Hunt High School was legally required to welcome me back. I was to be in touch with a school social worker each week, Mrs. Miller. She had short gray hair and wore gray suits; I remember her as monochrome. She had her own office in a separate wing of the school, away from the main office. I dutifully saw her at least once a week like I was supposed to, usually during my study hall.

It was now late September. I had been meeting with Mr. North for only a little while, once or twice a week after school. I wasn't yet writing *to* him, only *for* him. No matter how little I slept, I always made sure to eventually come to school so I could stay after with him and then drive my little sister home. But my attendance was still far from perfect.

Mr. North wouldn't comment on when I arrived. He wouldn't ask. He'd just sit next to me at his desk and we'd write together. And then we'd switch papers, circle and underline our favorite parts. Once, when he was waiting for me to finish reading, he took out a paper box tied with red-and-white bakery string. He began eating a series of Italian cookies, their sweet, sugar smell filling the classroom. I put my pencil down.

"Can I have one?"

"Have you finished?" He eyed his paper under my hand.

I pursed my mouth and sighed, turning back down to his page. I heard him chuckle. Then I felt his hand on my wrist, picking it up gently, like it was something delicate. He didn't look at me, just circled the bakery string around my wrist, tying it carefully under my hand. I watched his fingers, the hairs on his arm glowing from the afternoon sun. The bang of his door thrown open—

"Hey, sissy. Can we go home now?" Our bodies turned as Lauren stepped into the classroom. I had lost time entirely. I grabbed my paper and shoved it into my backpack, yelling goodbye to Mr. North as we began walking through the hallway.

In my car, Lauren tapped her fingers on the door frame, the quiet of the afternoon breezing in through the open window.

"He's really cute, Ali." She didn't look at me. I felt my skin go hot.

I kept one hand on the wheel and with the other pulled my hair over my shoulder, hiding my face from her. I glanced at my new string bracelet.

"Totally," I said as I turned on the radio. "How was tennis practice?" The subject of the teacher was dropped, and the day continued on. I didn't untie the bracelet that night, or the next day, or the next.

—

A few days later, Mrs. Miller asked me to come to her office, in the middle of classes. Our mandated meetings were usually Friday afternoons during my study hall, a week wind-down, she called it. This was not one of those meetings. I sat across from her, another large wooden desk between us. Big, curtainless windows behind her looked onto the school parking lot.

"We're going to figure this out, Alisson." She was always very positive. She didn't bring my file with her to our meetings, a nice gesture. "What's keeping you from getting to class in the morning? Dr. Williams isn't pleased you keep missing Latin."

There was only one Latin teacher in my high school. When I was a freshman, Dr. Williams adored me. I had taken Latin and etymology during a summer college program the previous summer and came in able to decline complex verbs by heart. He would pair me with students who struggled, which made me feel like an ally instead of a nerd. I loved the patterns of the words, all the myths and images of antiquity, how signs from goddesses could be scattered in everyday life. If you just paid enough attention, the answers would appear in the stars, would fall from the sky into your hands. I longed for that illumination. I longed for a lot of things as a teen girl.

But this was how my first day back at Latin class went a few weeks earlier:

I took a seat near the back of the classroom as the bells rang in succession, signaling the start of class. I recognized some of the other students, but no one more than in passing. Some glanced at me, blankly, and went back to each other.

Dr. Williams stood up from his desk and started his introductory routine as the third and final bell rang, his name on the chalkboard, greeting us in Latin, "*Salve,* seniors!" The not-so-silent groan from students as they remembered what high school was supposed to be about. He began calling out names from the class roster, assigning seats in a seemingly random order, not alphabetically by last name as many teachers did. I moved out of my seat to stand in the back of the room as the desk I had been sitting in was assigned, waiting to hear my name.

He implored us to remember these seats for the rest of the year, also in Latin, *"Caveat!"* and began writing a series of page numbers on the blackboard.

I was left sitting on the heating unit, the big bulk by the window. It wasn't on, it was August. But it wasn't a desk. My hand raised from the back of the room. "Dr. Williams?" I said. "I think you missed me."

He turned back and looked at me, an expression passed over his face.

"No, Alisson, I think we should see how the year goes," he said. He remembered me. "You can just take a seat in the back for now."

A silent room of teenagers. Twenty-something pairs of eyes on me, but no mouths moved as I took an open seat in the back row. The tick of the oversize clock on the wall. He started his lecture. I took out a freshly sharpened pencil and wrote down nearly everything he said for the next forty-four minutes, desperate. Eventually the bell rang again, class was over. Twenty-something teenagers rushing out. I flipped back to the front page of the notebook and wrote, on the inside of the cover, in neat, straight lines: *This year will be different. I will show him. I will show everyone.*

I had that notebook in my backpack as Mrs. Miller asked me again, "What's going on?" I focused on the cars through the window behind her; it was raining that day and it wasn't foggy or anything but they all looked sort of misty, none of the colors were bright like in some spring rains. It was fully fall. Browns and yellows and reds, even in the rain. There were wet leaves everywhere now. Dr. Williams would barely look at me, even when I was in class in my unassigned seat on time. The attendance secretaries sighed when they saw me walk in the office. Most days I skipped lunch and just wandered the side hallways of the school because I didn't have anyone to sit with and didn't want to call attention to that any more than I already did with my very existence.

I *hated* crying in front of people. I had done so much of it for so long already and I was tired of it, the way people just stare at you or start talking way too fast and always try to touch you, as if your shoulder is where it hurts. But I couldn't help it—I couldn't help it all those years when I constantly wished I were dead, and I couldn't help it that afternoon either.

Mrs. Miller didn't speed up her questions, she didn't invade my sad space. She placed a box of Kleenex in front of me and stood up to look at a book on her shelf, leaving me to the tissues. Once I got to the point of sniffling, she sat back down. She asked me if I was ready to talk. I told her about the women in the office, about how I didn't know what I was doing wrong with Latin class, I was doing all the homework, and I always did really well on the quizzes, and how I thought lunch was a stupid period. She nodded, made some notes on a yellow pad she kept on her desk. "Okay, Alisson. Let's see what we can make happen."

By the following week I had a new morning routine: I was no longer to be buzzed in through the main office if I was late. Instead, I was to go to Mrs. Miller's window and tap three times. If I stood on my tiptoes, my knuckles just met the glass. She would knock back. Then she would meet me at the side door at the end of her hallway and let me in, and she would report to the attendance monitors for me. If she was in a meeting or something and couldn't tap back, I just had to knock on the window next to hers, all the guidance counselors were in on it. I'd say hi and check in about how I slept or didn't and she'd write me a hall pass to get wherever I was supposed to be. And it was officially official.

And I had an assigned desk in Latin. It was in the back still, but it was mine.

That same week, Mr. North found me wandering the halls for the first time. A quick wave, asking for a hall pass I didn't have but joking about my empty hands instead of sending me to the principal's office. Then he saw me the next day. And then again, and this time he asked where I was supposed to be.

"Lunch?" I shuffled my backpack to my other shoulder.

"Aren't you hungry?" he asked as I leaned against lockers while he talked. I tried not to meet his face.

I wrinkled my nose. "The only thing worth eating in there are the french fries."

I made him laugh. He brushed my shoulder with his hand, my eyes following the moment of contact the whole time, that same alive and electric flash, and told me to meet him in the cafeteria later—he monitored the fourth lunch shift, we needed to talk about that poem I gave him yesterday anyway.

"Would you be kind enough to join me?" He made a faux bow, tipped an invisible hat, and I smiled for the first time that day. He just wanted me there for my french fries, he told me. What else did I have that he could want?

5

I had always wanted to be someone else. Anyone else. I hated myself and my life and would sometimes stare at my pet cat and wish I could be him instead. Wish I could live a life of endless naps instead of burying my head when my alarm went off, of whiskers and claws instead of scars and secrets. So, naturally, I wanted to be an actress. Where the entire point is to be another person completely.

Ever since my breakout role as a speaking Munchkin in my elementary school production of *The Wizard of Oz*, a coup for a first grader if there ever was one, I knew I had what it took to be on the stage. I had performed in Shakespeare plays multiple times by my senior year, shining as Witch #2 in *Macbeth* and as Hermia in *A Midsummer Night's Dream*, embracing the unnamed role of "Wench" in various Elizabethan romantic comedies. So when the fall play was announced at Hunt, my name was top of the list to audition. And that was before I knew the teacher was codirecting.

Mr. North took great interest in my interest in doing the play. He offered his directorial critique of my audition the week before, which was a big deal. While we were already meeting most days to write, or really just talk, that time shifted to memorizing lines and him telling me how to express my inner desires through the way I held my hands. Our afternoons were full of make-believe.

It's not like he gave any of his other students this kind of attention, he told me. But I wanted the part and he wanted to help. I was so lucky.

I decided to audition with Emily's monologue from *Our Town*, all goodbye world and looking and Grover's Corners. He watched me perform it in his classroom, an audience of one, already memorized, like a professional. He was writing the whole time, his eyes up and down from the paper. I finished with real tears.

"Well?" I asked.

He coughed and gave me what he had been writing—I was elated and racing and then I started reading. He wholly redirected me, in two pages of notes, full of:

X rt. @ everything . . . point to yourself @ "look @ me" . . . Sunflowers-pantomime smelling one, "Oh earth"— grab-full out—to audience

I knew he knew better than me. So I did my best to ignore my instincts. His notes were so specific, I had been doing everything wrong before. And at times, those afternoons in his classroom, it felt as though he was directing *me*, not just me as Emily Webb.

> *@ sigh [stage direction]*
> *Collect yourself*
> *Stand up*
> *Brush yourself off*
> *Look poised*

It seemed like he wanted that for me more than just on-stage. Like it was a directive for my life, even—*things have been hard but you can stand up and collect yourself and look poised while you do it.* No one else in my life thought I was capable of something like that.

The last time we practiced with all his changes, he stood up from his chair and clapped.

"That was beautiful, Ali." He had begun calling me Ali. "You nailed it."

"Thanks," I said as I wrung my hands. "But will Mr. Ulman think so?" Mr. Ulman was not only the director of the school play but also my theater teacher and my honors English teacher. Sometimes when I did an improv in class, he would lean back in the audience, monologue about what good choices I was making onstage. I knew that meant he liked me. Sometimes in English class when he called on me, I knew I had the right answer, and his nod and tight smile told me so. But when I came in late to either class, he would sigh, loud enough for me to hear. When I missed class entirely,

Mr. Ulman would look between my eyes when I asked for the homework assignment and speak without stopping as I tried to get it down.

"I'll fight for you. You deserve this," Mr. North assured me. "He trusts me. I never failed him." Mr. Ulman had been the teacher's own teacher ten years ago, when Mr. North had been a student at Hunt himself. He regaled me with stories about his starring role as Jesus in their production of *Jesus Christ Superstar*, just how awesome he was. I had no doubts.

I practiced my monologue aloud yet again as I drove home, Lauren following along on the printout and correcting me when I made a mistake.

The next day was the big audition. And then the following was the second round, where it was me against another girl, Christina—younger, but she was talented and knew it. Now we had to read monologues from the script of *Inherit the Wind*. There was only one real female role, Rachel. The teacher whispered to me in the entrance of the auditorium as I walked in, as part of my interior backstory and motivation, "She's easily manipulated." I nodded back.

I tried to think of ways to show manipulation in the reading aloud of only a few sentences—should I cry? and then stop crying? seem confused with what to do with my arms?—and came to no satisfactory conclusion.

Christina auditioned. Then it was my turn. I decided to try crying and see if performing pain would get me the part. Crying onstage was easy—I felt like crying a lot of the time anyway, so it was just a matter of bottling it up for the day, popping the cork in front of others. Performing the pain didn't lessen it, though. Crying in public just made it harder for others to ignore.

The next day, a piece of paper tacked onto a hallway bulletin board, the cast list: I got the part. I screamed and spun around to find the teacher and tell him and—there he was, waiting for me.

"I wanted to tell you myself," he said. "I convinced Mr. Ulman you could do this." He reached across the space between our bodies and touched my arm. Skin on skin. My eyes wide as I stared back at him.

I was suddenly overwhelmed by the urge to kiss him. Like a flash in my mind—the image of me reaching across space and pushing my toes into the ground to rise up and press my mouth against his. A moment of make-believe. I shook my head a little and coughed and thanked him. Everything felt hot and prickly. I knew I got cast because of him, because he vouched for me, he put himself on the line for me. It seemed like no one had done anything like that for me in a long time. It was like my prince had come.

6

Things escalated quickly. By October, I was spending time alone with Mr. North nearly every school day, either right after school or at night. Sometimes both. There wasn't always enough time for him to read my journal after school anymore, with all the preparation for the play, so we began meeting late at night at the diner to have time to talk about my writing. He would read my journal from the day while I ate fries one by one and sipped lukewarm coffee. In school, he was always Mr. North; when we were alone at the diner, he became Nick.

Sometimes when I was going to meet him, I would tell my parents I was working that night and leave right after I got home, driving aimlessly for a few hours before going to the diner. My mother didn't know my schedule, after all. Other times I said I was going to meet a friend, someone I hadn't actually spoken with in months. Or sometimes I said I was going somewhere to work on a paper. I don't think I was a very good liar. I didn't ask why there weren't any questions. I was happy to be out of the house.

—

I had begun writing *to* Mr. North, directly, invoking a "you" on the pages of my journals. He told me the second person was a really personal, intimate way to write. Wasn't I writing to him when we were together anyway? Which had become more often—he had begun giving me hall passes to come into his classroom even when he was teaching, so he could make sure I was dedicating myself to my writing. To him.

Even in Ms. Croix's class, in our official composition book, which she read every weekend, where I had to be conscious and careful, I found myself writing about him anyway.

For a prompt in class, I wrote:

*October 8th, *10 Things That Make Me Happy*:*
1. My cats—Sampson, George, and Lilly
2. Getting the part I wanted in the play.
3. Going to a diner and sitting.

I couldn't help it—he made me happy. Which I hadn't been in a long time.

Our first out-of-school meeting was by accident, just running into each other at the local coffee shop. Sitting at tables next to each other. Meeting at the diner in the evenings was a natural extension. The plan appeared in conversation one afternoon, as he began putting his notebooks into his messenger bag in his empty classroom.

"Well, we've gotten a lot done with the monologue, but we don't have time now to talk about your writing." Another book into his bag. "I'm probably going to want some disco fries later tonight," he said, which I knew meant he was going to the diner.

As we walked down the quiet hall, seemingly the only ones in the whole school, he continued: "I don't like Blue Sky—it's crawling with teenagers. Have you ever been to the Olympia Diner?" Sure, I assured him. I went home and fixed my makeup, ate dinner with my mom and sister, and left again, journal in hand. I shouted something about meeting someone to study with as I walked out the door.

I got there by 7:00 P.M. Took the back booth, facing the doors. Ordered a coffee. A refill. Another. My hands shaking as I slurped the hot, bitter liquid. And then, there he was, walking toward me.

"Well, what are the chances of this?" he said as our eyes met across the diner. What a coincidence.

Then he began asking me out, for real. In his classroom, while his students were supposed to be reading something, he would be writing the next prompt on the board. He told me in advance, as the bell ended its ring, signaling class was starting, to pay attention. He'd meet my eyes, write the number 9 on the board, circle it, erase it. The intensity of my focus on him made me dizzy, watching and waiting for the signs to appear. I knew this language.

I was always, always on time for him, if not early. But some nights he would be later than he thought or have to bring things to grade and we wouldn't really get to talk.

I'd occasionally help him read a student's essay and tell him what number I thought it deserved. He usually agreed with my assessment. "You'll make a great teacher someday, Ali." I beamed.

We passed notes across the booth like we were in someone else's classroom. Sometimes we'd write a poem together, each writing a line back and forth. He'd circle the parts he liked, I'd copy those stray lines into my journal, since I knew I couldn't keep anything we wrote. *Keeping it a secret makes it special*, he wrote to me on a napkin, blue ink bleeding where he underlined *special*. I nodded because I knew what he was risking for this, for me: his job. I began writing in my creative writing journals, over and over, *I will not be his pink slip. I will not be his pink slip.*

Ms. Croix continued collecting my journals every few weeks for her class throughout the rest of the year. I don't know what she thought that meant or what she thought of anything else I wrote. I don't know what my answer would have been if she'd asked me. I have only my memories and my journals to know what I thought—*I will not be his pink slip.* Sometimes even underlined. I was so sure about that.

7

This is a scene I didn't know had happened:

I had therapy every week, almost an hour's drive away. Most weeks my mother would drive me. We'd play punch buggy on the drive, the updated Volkswagen Beetle being brand new and seemingly everywhere, a car she had had herself as a teenager. We kept score into the hundreds, me usually ahead. I spotted the bright colors faster, it seemed.

I didn't tell my therapist about the teacher. If I did mention him, it was in the same way I mentioned him to Mrs. Miller at school: he's nice, he spends time with me, I think he's so smart. Maybe I blushed sometimes, but I didn't tell them what was actually happening. In my sessions, I would pick off my nail polish, usually black or a sparkly blue, letting the bits of shellac fall to the carpet at the edge of the couch. She must have had to pick them up after I left every time. I never thought about it that way, then. I just wanted something to do with my hands.

After I had my fifty-minute session, my mother would go into my therapist's office and chat for a few minutes. Nothing to break confidentiality, but just to check in. Sometimes I was there for that too.

—

One time, early in the fall, my mother brought up to my therapist, in an after-session chat, that she thought I was staying out too late, wasn't being honest about who I was with, and she wasn't sure of the best way to handle it. I was getting to school, after all. I wasn't suicidal anymore. I seemed to be doing better in so many ways.

I can imagine my therapist removing her glasses and pinching the bridge of her nose, like she often did before she spoke after listening for a long time. "Janice, just let her be a teenager. Do you think she is in any danger?"

My mother said she didn't. So they agreed—leave it be. If real problems arise, they'll be dealt with. In the meantime, she told my mother, cut her some slack.

8

I was beautiful in high school. I don't know why that is so hard to admit, but it is.

Acknowledging the fact that I was attractive as a teenager feels shameful, the dirtiest of secrets, something you should never say openly. Yet anyone looking at a photograph of me at seventeen would see what I do now—clear, fair skin; big, blue eyes; long, dark hair; the beginnings of an hourglass shape. If a boy had a crush on me, flirtations would often allude to how I looked like a Disney princess. (And I did, if princesses wore jeans and black nail polish.) I look back at photographs from twenty years ago and see it plain: I was pretty.

Prettiness is complicated. Not acknowledging this feels like a lie of omission, sidestepping something important. But being pretty didn't make me any more or less vulnerable. Being pretty didn't keep me from being suicidal when I was fifteen and sixteen, it didn't stop me from making bad choices about where I placed my trust. It didn't make me easier prey. But maybe it made me stand out.

At seventeen, I was deeply insecure and convinced I was not capable of being loved, and also certain that my body was my only possible source of power. I held both of these beliefs tightly, one in each hand. One did not discount the other. I knew that my only chance of getting what I wanted, more than anything—to be noticed, to feel like I was in control of some part of my life—was through being attractive.

This was the early aughts. Britney Spears had already asked for it one more time, Christina Aguilera stripped on MTV, even Fiona Apple writhed in underwear for her music videos. Stores like Abercrombie & Fitch sold short-short skirts by the thousands at suburban malls like the ones I roamed, jeans were so low that bikini waxes were considered necessary, and push-up bras filled the racks of Victoria's Secret. The casual coverage of grunge clothes—oversize flannels, ripped tights, long prairie skirts—were *so* not cool anymore. To be pretty meant a certain amount of conscious, overt effort—the eye-liner, the glossy lips, the tanning booths—but you couldn't *look* like you were trying. Then you were just trashy, a joke. I never wanted to be that.

—

I knew the teacher thought I was pretty. I *knew*. I knew from the way he watched me after school, when I was sitting right next to him, never touching, around the corner of his big desk. That kind of institutional school furniture that looks heavy and hard, unmoving. I began to feel from across the desk how his body would move in response to mine, like magnets doing the wrong thing. A sort of pressing.

He would say something nice about what I wore, especially if it was something from Abercrombie instead of a big flannel, like I usually wore. The tight T-shirts showed off my "shape," as he would say. A shiver ran through me when he said those things, and I'd try to stand up a little taller, elongate my neck, and push down my shoulders, make my body look as feminine and sultry as possible.

"You're very shapely today," he said, his voice hushed as I walked through his classroom door. He'd continue on paper about how he wanted to know all about those shapes, he should go back to geometry class to learn. *And what grade do you think you would get?* I countered. Written back: *I was an honor roll student. Go check my permanent record.* And he winked at me as he slid the paper to me.

The teacher would comment on my perfume, a slow-moving oil called Egyptian Goddess that I would roll behind my ears every morning. "Nice, Ali." If someone else was there, it was *Miss Wood* this, *Miss Wood* that. But alone, it was Ali. Sometimes Alice, like from *Alice's Adventures in Wonderland*. He admonished me for not having read the book, for only watching the Disney cartoon, for not knowing my supposed namesake better.

"I don't think my parents named me after Alice in Wonderland," I told him. He disagreed, explaining how names worked and how they were all connected to the original Old English names. So how, know it or not, my parents *were* naming me after Alice. Just like his parents named him after the Catholic saint. Nick. How I should *always* call him Nick, when we were alone.

"Oh." I twirled my hair and pressed my lips together, rewetting my lip gloss. I had no idea about those things. I thought you just picked a name you liked. I didn't realize their power.

9

I didn't know what college would mean for me. Graduating from high school at all still seemed far away and uncertain—planning the next step seemed a fantasy. As a girl, I thumb-tacked pennants from Harvard, Columbia, to my bedroom walls; debated the merits of New York University's Tisch Drama School versus Juilliard. I spent my summers practic-ing Shakespeare for theater auditions, memorizing lyrics to musicals, doing dance steps over and over in the backyard to get them right before going onstage. I thought about being an actress, or a lawyer, starting a charity to help children, or maybe writing novels that won lots of awards. Now, I knew those dreams weren't going to be a reality anytime soon. I just wanted to get through high school.

I had always wanted to go to New York City for college. I lived close enough that it was only a train ride away, Broad-way and real museums and places where artists breathed. My parents let me go to an open house event at the School of

Visual Arts, unchaperoned. It was like a tiny field trip, with another student in my creative writing class, David, and me. I had been in NYC lots of times before, but this time it felt different when we walked through Grand Central Terminal, looking up at the painted stars, took the subway to the Flatiron District, and walked through the city streets. We got a coffee at a small shop called Insomniac. The customers wore flannel shirts and dark-rimmed glasses and everyone seemed to have a book in their lap and a notebook on the table.

At the open house, as the admissions counselor clicked through a series of slides giving examples of good and bad submissions—the weirder the better, it seemed—David and I whispered back and forth about the shape of the lines and the colors and what we thought it meant. What it would be like to be so creative all the time. The administrator was in a black dress with black tights and black Doc Martens, but with tortoiseshell glasses and blue nail polish. Her hair matched her nails. Everyone listened to her, taking notes. She was the kind of person I wanted to be.

I came back from the visit encouraged—the School of Visual Arts didn't care so much about your grades, although they did a little, but it was about your potential as an artist, as a creative person. I was pure potential at that point, and even though drawing wasn't my best outlet, I had always done lots of mixed-medium work and painted. The examples they showed on a slideshow, the prospective student administrator clicking along, weren't even necessarily that good—they weren't Rembrandts, they were focused on *saying something*. I could do that. I had lots to say.

I thought about what a portfolio could look like for me, how I could maybe incorporate some of my poems with paint. And I kept looking at the audition slots for Juilliard and Tisch; maybe I could be good enough to be a real actress. I knew I needed something different for college, maybe designing my own curriculum was the answer, one of those colleges with no majors or grades. I applied to Bennington College with that in mind and signed up for an overnight visit. I also hedged my bets and applied to Manhattanville College, a semi-local smaller school that was likely to take me even with my checkered transcript on the merits of my high SAT scores (in English, at least) and a good essay. I wrote about dealing with depression and having electroconvulsive therapy, how I knew these past few years hadn't been the most successful but I was better now and determined to change my life and be something my future alma mater could be proud of.

I told Mr. North about my plans. He just sort of nodded, offered to look at my essay. "Have you considered Ithaca?" he asked. I had not. He started going on about his experience at Cornell University, upstate in Ithaca, New York. How beautiful it was, how it changed his life, how he got to go to Oxford and study Charles Dickens and it was just the best thing ever.

"Well, I don't really think I'm about to get into Cornell," I said. I was drawing endless stars in my journal as I listened to him. We had had a conversation the other night about Shakespeare and his star-crossed lovers.

"Yeah, but maybe you could get into Ithaca College," he

offered. He told me all the prettiest girls in Ithaca were there, that's how it was, and the Cornell guys dated the Ithaca College girls. "I'm thinking about going back next year to get my Ph.D."

My pen stopped. My eyes slowly met his. "Oh?" I said.

"Yeah, I just want more, you know? I'm not going to be a teacher forever." I pushed on my mouth from the inside. I had to meet Mrs. Miller and was almost late, the second bell was about to ring.

"Huh," I said super casually as I gathered my things into my black backpack. "Well, see you later." I smiled as he waved.

I took a detour before I went into Mrs. Miller's office, which was right next to the guidance office. They had a wall of shiny, colorful brochures from colleges across the country, nearly floor to ceiling of names and pictures of smiling students and beautiful views. I found Ithaca College. I took a pamphlet, checked the application dates. I could still make it.

10

Lolita came into my life before the first snowfall. The trees were still holding tight to their leaves, desperate to keep from changing. I was perfect. I was a mess. I called to him, he would later say. I was one of Poe's Annabel sirens, one of Odysseus's distractions, sad and singing, longing for someone. Needing to be pulled apart by someone who knew better. I can see that now, my girl-self refracted through time and distance, through space.

Now, there is a poem that echoes when I think about the teacher and that time. It is by Margaret Atwood. When I was seventeen I had never even heard of Margaret Atwood. I had read only Sylvia Plath, over and over, her bell jar ringing everywhere in my world.

Margaret Atwood wrote, *This is the one song everyone would like to learn: the song that is irresistible.* I was voracious in my longing, in my loneliness. I asked for it, for him. I begged. I wanted to learn. But even still, I was sincere in my

budding grief for my child body. My body was actively be-
traying me with hips, menstruation, stretch marks like purple marker on my breasts, all of the things that shifted the
way men looked at me. If this *was* power, I wasn't sure it was
worth it. I wanted the safety of childhood *and* the power of
sex. I wanted it all, in my life and in my body.

—

The teacher gave me the book in the parking lot of the Olympia Diner, late October, *Lolita*. The cover was a black-and-
white photograph of a girl's legs, spinning in saddle shoes
and a skirt. No one looked at us in the parking lot; there
was no one to look. It was evening and dark and if I was late
going home, my parents might notice. I should have been
home. Our cars were parked next to each other, but I hadn't
been inside his yet—a lease, a Volkswagen Jetta, navy blue,
new. It was so cool compared with my old brown Saab, wal-
nut brown if I'm being complimentary. John Mayer crooned
from Mr. North's stereo system.

He told me it would blow my mind, reading Nabokov,
that I would never be the same after. He read me the opening, cars on the highway behind us. I rested my hip on my
car door, stars and streetlights in the side mirror. The mirror
was spotted and hazy. *In my arms she was always Lolita.* He
touched my arm with the back of his finger. Just for a second,
but everything came alive inside me and I was sure. I knew
what I wanted.

11

The series of bells became our song—the first meant I could go to him; the middle that I was almost there, a warning that if I didn't hurry, I would get caught in the hallway and be given a detention slip; the third that I was inside his classroom, a ring of safety. He wrote me hall passes to forgive my late arrivals to my other classes, to excuse my absences, checking the box *Excused from Class*, filling in the blank *Reason: Writing Extra Help*. Or checking *Admit to Class* or *Accept Excuse*. It was all code from teacher to teacher. The date, the time, the room number: 11/11, A105, 11:27 A.M.

He would sign his name with a flourish on the passes, always in green ink, impressing me with his pen. Sometimes he would use nicknames for other teachers, "To: Josucks" instead of Mr. Josephs. Once I asked him why—my fingers around my thumbs as I looked from the clock face to his, the clock face again. My book bag was heavy. I was *so* late.

"Teachers are not always Mr. or Miss, y'know," he said as he capped his green fountain pen, as if he were trying to teach me something. "They're more than just your teacher."

I looked back at him as I left his classroom.

—

My other teachers must have noticed that I always had official excuses from Mr. North for being late or leaving class early, but no one looked beyond the pieces of paper. I wasn't ever pressed with a question in the hallway that his signed pass couldn't answer.

Once, I was sitting in his classroom, there was morning sunshine still from the windows but the floor was cold. November, no snow days yet. I was supposed to be somewhere else. Our usual arrangement in his rectangle room: him, teaching at the blackboard; his students, in rows of desks facing the board; me, sitting against the bookshelf on the back wall, between the wall and his desk, my books and papers spread out on the floor. None of the students ever questioned why there was a girl sitting back there. I'm not sure how often they even noticed—they'd have to stand up, turn around, and be at a certain angle from their seats to see me. But Mr. North, when he looked at his students, could look right at me. It was a tenth-grade English class. They didn't know my name; they didn't care.

I was reading the book, the Nabokov, "the only convincing love story of our century," said *Vanity Fair* on the cover. This was the teacher's copy, with his notes, I had to take care.

I didn't realize until later that he had inscribed it to me, in green flourish:

> *To Alisson,*
> *This book is lust, yearning, and occupational hazards.*
> *And lightning.*
> *Enjoy.*
>
> *—N.N.*

I moved along in the text, already to chapter 11, Humbert Humbert's pocket diary of watching his nymphet. I didn't know what the word meant the first time—something to do with a nymph, that mythical being? I asked Mr. North, and he told me to look in *The Oxford English Dictionary*. Actually, he said the *OED*, and when I got to the library to find it, they had only *Webster's*. I learned it was from the Greek and Latin (*nympha*) but was still a bit perplexed by its usage. Other than the mythical association, it suggested immature insects. Adolescent butterflies. I *knew* it was sexy, it couldn't be more obvious from the surrounding language, but what was so sexy about a teenage creature? That stage between larva and adulthood, between a baby and grown-up. As someone currently in that stage, I thought it sucked. But whenever the teacher mentioned it, in passing, in reference to me, I just smiled back and played along.

Chapter 11 of *Lolita* was Humbert's calendar of viewing his nymphet. *Saturday . . . Glimpse of shiny skin between T-shirt and white gym shorts. Bending . . .* A dorsal view, as Humbert called it, as Mr. North underlined. I thought this was referencing a sea creature at first, maybe a part of a dolphin? It wasn't until I found the word again, old, reliable *Webster's*, that I turned red.

Mr. North had copied down another review of the Nabokov novel on the title page, as if to remind me what this was: *highbrow pornographic trash*. He told me once, in the diner, "The beauty is in the twinning of the porn and the love story," in between eating fistfuls of french fries. I shook my head in muddled confusion and wrote it down on a napkin. And then watched it dissipate in water before we left. But writing it made me remember.

That day in November, in his classroom, I was watching his hands, chalk white on his fingers. I was waiting for him to write the number for later that night. He hadn't written one yet. I looked at the clock—only a minute before the first bell, the beginning of the end of class. In the previous chapter of *Lolita*, I had underlined *And there she is there, lost in the middle, gnawing a pencil, detested by teachers, all the boys' eyes on her hair and neck,* my *Lolita*. I felt like no one noticed that I was there, on the floor. Not the other kids, not the other teachers, not even Mr. North. I thought about his hands. I imagined taking one along my shirt, wiping the chalk off, I imagined kissing the top of his thumb where he had a callus from playing guitar. He told me he was writing a new song about a crush he had the other afternoon, I hoped it was about me. I imagined biting it, I imagined pressing my tongue against his thumb. I thought how he hadn't written a number today and I had been sitting on the concrete floor for forty minutes now.

I thought about what Lolita would do. *Glimpse of shiny skin.*
I turned around.

By then I had scooted over far enough behind his desk. In
the slight shadow between it and the blue cinder-block wall,
I knew that none of the students could see me. I didn't look
at the teacher anymore. I leaned over, deeply, into the book,
now facing the windows, still on my knees, my back to him. I
knew that as I delved into the pages he had given me, the upper edge of my black lace underwear, bought with my father's
credit card, would creep above the back of my low-rise jeans,
that when Mr. North turned to address his students, I was all
that he would see, a strip of skin.

Once, at night, at the diner, he wrote about my age, how
wrong it all was that we shouldn't be together—*girls who are
only eighteen are in* Playboy *and we are told to look and then
you*—. He didn't finish the thought, even on a paper place
mat. But he showed it to me. I understood at that moment in
his classroom on my knees how Lolita worked her magic on
Humbert. *This must be what power feels like.*

The first bell rang. The ambient noise of chairs moving,
backpacks closing, papers, books, pencils, all preparing to go.
I heard his voice, the homework assignment repeated to no
one in particular. I heard the other noises fade, his footsteps
close, then stop. I arched my back and slowly sat up, tossed
my long, dark hair. I twisted it around with my hand; the
other still held my place in Nabokov. *That glimpse of shiny
skin.* I felt like it had been quiet for hours in the waiting for
him, for his words, not just on paper, not just chalk. I looked
back toward him over my shoulder, he leaned down into me.

This was the closest his mouth had ever come to me. I felt the heat of his blood against my cheek.

"You are so sexy," he said. I met his gaze. And the warning bell rang.

12

At what point does a man transform into a wolf? In fairy tales and myths, the change seems instant. A wicked witch points, a god nods. Poof. There may be some smoke and sulfur. Or just the knowledge that things are no longer the same. A man has become something dangerous.

I thought I was something powerful in this story. Lip gloss and low-rise jeans, low enough that if I reached up for something, my tummy would be exposed, I was someone who could make the rules.

Please come in, I beckoned. My house is so empty, I would love some company. Lips wet. The door shuts behind us both.

In the real world, transformation happens so slowly, softly, that it is rarely seen. A ripening of fruit to something edible from a cold pit, a shift in the way someone looks at you. But just the same as in the fairy tales and myths, all at once things are irreparably different.

On November 20, the teacher asked me what my bra size was. During his study hall, held in the woodshop classroom, the notes we passed back and forth.

You know you're really pretty. I scrunched my nose and looked at him. The warm wood all around us. Even today I smell fresh sawdust and there I am, seventeen, afternoon light pouring through the back wall of windows in that classroom. Dust on my palms if I press them against one of the benches.

Really, he wrote. *A classic hourglass. That tiny waist.*

I held back my smile and felt red creep across my skin.

What's your bra size? I bet you're a solid C.

Everything dropped inside me, my heart louder than ever before. *Pardon?* I wrote back.

C'mon. Don't be coy with me.

I just shook my head, too hard, protesting too much.

I'll trade you.

For what?

You tell me yours, I'll tell you mine. He looked right at me as he pressed the paper to my fingers.

My heart was louder than ever before. I was sure he could hear it, that it was beating through the whole room.

Tell me what? I played it cool. Looked up at him.

Oh, you know. Don't you want to?

Everything banging around inside my body. I looked back up at him. Remembered to breathe.

Trade? he wrote. *I'll find out anyway. Don't keep me waiting.*

I reached out my pinkie finger. He latched his over mine and shook.

32C.

7¾.

I realized I didn't actually know what that number meant. *Is that a lot for a penis?* I asked myself. I wasn't a virgin, but it's not like before sex I took out my trusty ruler. If he was telling me, though, that must be a big deal.

Wow! I wrote back. Underlined it twice.

He smiled at me. *Yeah*, and drew a smiley face too. *I can't wait for you.*

I drew a smile back. The bell rang, and he ripped up the paper we had been passing back and forth. Small enough pieces like snow that he let fall into the wastepaper basket next to broken pieces of wood. I collected my things slowly, as the bells continued to ring and make me feel small. I was going to be late. He knew, wrote me a hall pass, 11/20 12:35, sent me on my way to creative writing class. I pressed my books to my chest and left the classroom, giggling like a schoolgirl who knew too much. I couldn't believe he trusted me with something so *private*.

At what point does a girl turn into prey?

13

Dear reader, if it seems like this is all happening awful fast, that's because it did. Within a matter of weeks I went from feeling utterly alone to being cast as the lead in the school play; my writing not only encouraged but admired; having someone I knew I could turn to, someone who made me feel safe, even in the halls of my high school. And all of this was because of him. My teacher, my knight in shining armor, my secret admirer. Mr. North. Nick. Now I coasted along campus carefree, no matter the time, because of the power in my hall pass. It kept me from getting in trouble, but it was also a constant reminder of Mr. North in my hand, something I could hold, the little slip of paper that had my name and *his* on it. Together. A concrete representation of the teacher's care for me, of his concern. How he could protect me. *Secrets are safe*, he would say to me, write to me, whisper before I left the room. I had never felt like that before in high school. I had always felt like I was being watched, hunted even. Now I felt like no one could reach me. Like I was finally safe.

14

Weekends at Rhapsody in Brew, the local café. Whenever the teacher had a gig in town, playing guitar and singing his own songs and covers, too, I was there. Sometimes I was the first one. I tried to be cool, take my time at the coffee bar, smiling at the guy behind the register as I smoothed my hair. The teacher didn't notice, though. I wasn't the only girl there.

While our afternoons after school and late nights at the diner were just us, his shows would be packed with other students. Mostly girls, but guys would come too. The girls thought he was *so cute*, the boys thought he was *so cool*. His dark hair and easy smile, former quarterback for the Hunt football team. Something for everyone.

Almost all of my previous boyfriends in high school had played guitar. I'd know we were really in love because they'd write a song for me, not just sing Dave Matthews Band's "Crash Into Me," Edwin McCain's "I'll Be," or "Glycerine" by Bush as they looked into my eyes when we were alone in their bedroom. They'd compose something themselves, put details about our first date or something secret in the words they sang. That's how I'd know it was real.

The teacher hadn't written a song for me yet. But sometimes when he'd be singing at those shows, his hands moving around the neck of his guitar and strumming the body, he'd look right at me, into my eyes, and it was like we were alone again. My whole body would go gooseflesh and soft when he did that.

After his sets, which were usually a few songs, he'd put his guitar away and sit, let a student buy him a coffee, and he'd go on about his artistic choices about that song he sang to the group of students that surrounded him, how it was all a metaphor for desire. Enraptured doesn't even begin to describe how I'd feel when he'd do that.

Whenever I'd see him next, I'd go on about how good he was, have to swallow a lot because just remembering it would make my body feel liquid again. He'd be demure about it, "Nah, it was just me playing around." But he was glad I came. Though I'd never get to really talk to him at his gigs, and it was like everyone there was more important than me. Once I asked him why he basically ignored me there, and he told me it was because it couldn't be obvious how much he cared about me—"We have to keep all this between us, remember?"

I understood, so I'd always say it was fine, "yeah, totally." But whenever I saw him talking to another girl, I couldn't help but feel hot and tight, all at once imagine him meeting her at a different diner the nights he didn't see me, wondering what he was writing to her. When that happened I'd shut my eyes and breathe in, out, and say over and over inside, *It's just me it's just me it's just me.* That this was happening only because I was *that* special, that he would never risk his job like this for any other girl. That I was the only one for him. I believed him. It would be years before I found out that wasn't true. That it wasn't about being special at all.

15

So far, this is a story about looking. All of this, the extended seduction, the lines not yet crossed, the temptation, the imagined, mimicking Nabokov's *Lolita*. This part of the story is about the gaze and what it felt like in my body to look at someone who looked back at me, to see and be seen. All I wanted was to be seen. To be acknowledged, to be understood. To feel that connection when eyes meet and communication is instant without a word.

This is also a story about boundaries. An image in a mirror, a looking glass—you reach out and there's something between you and the other side. You're trapped on your side. You can only see the reflection of you. And what you're looking at isn't always real.

16

In Latin we conjugated on demand. Desks lined up like obedient children, Dr. Williams was unyielding but also kind in his efforts to make us say *salve*. It was still November, we were on the third declension, he had begun to no longer ignore me in class (now that I had been in class for two months straight). He remembered who I used to be and kept looking for her. He had short white hair and wore bow ties, he had an essay he wrote that was published in *The New York Times* about how Latin is "hip" framed right by the door. He called my name.

"Alisson! *Dolor!*"

I stood and started with the nominative for suffering, a unit of pain, "*Dolor, dolores, doloris, dolorum*," and continued through the vocative, singular, and plural confidently. In all my struggles, Latin was never one. Even with a year in French while I was at the therapeutic day school, Latin was latched into my mind and my mouth.

He nodded, I sat back down and began doodling *dolor*,

dolores, pain, in my notebook. Something was ringing inside. I drew hearts and rewrote it, *dolores,* in script, and again, a ringing. *Dolores. Dolores! Lolita's real name is Dolores!* I thought I could impress Mr. North later with this new definition, I could imagine, "So Lolita's actual name is Latin for *suffering,* isn't that, like fascinating?" The hop skip from Dolores to Lolita, from sadness to sex. Something was still ringing.

I thought I knew about sadness. I had broken up with plenty of boyfriends by then, been broken up with as well. I had gotten bad grades, been passed over for parts I wanted in a show, failed at plenty of things. But more than the everyday, I knew something darker.

I had spent a lot of my life depressed and had been in and out of therapists' and psychiatrists' offices for years. One of my favorite therapists had a jar of sugar-covered lemon drops on his desk. Another psychiatrist wore suits two sizes too big, his neck ping-ponging within his large collar when he discussed the next pill to try. Over the years, I had been on more than twenty medications, ranging from Prozac to lithium. When I had ECT, I had hated the simple fact that I was undergoing *shock therapy* so much that it outweighed the fact that it was making me better. I made lists of all the famous people and writers who had been depressed and had ECT, and taped them to my walls: Carrie Fisher, Vivien Leigh, Judy Garland, Virginia Woolf, Sylvia Plath. I read *The Bell Jar* like peeking into my own journal, the one I couldn't write in because everything was so hard. I felt kindred to writers like Plath. She too was drowning in her own sadness.

Lolita's name is sadness. Something about this fact circled inside me, in the cage of my chest, but it would be years before I could define it. It would be years before I understood the connection between Lolita, pain, and me.

17

Even though Mr. North had read easily a hundred pages of my writing by now (I had already filled three journals written directly *to* him, as instructed, plus all the other journals I filled, some for myself, some for Ms. Croix, I was always endlessly writing), we had never specifically, explicitly, spoken about my past. I had alluded to things in my entries, lines about darkness and anxieties, and wore short-sleeved shirts so the sun saw the scars on my arms, quiet reminders that I had been a cutter. But still. It was never discussed.

I was in Mr. North's classroom alone, waiting for him to come back from wherever he was, writing like the good student I wanted to be.

I heard the classroom door open and suddenly he was next to me and had put a form on the desk in front of me, asking me what it meant that I wasn't on it. It was a ballot for the teachers to complete, for Best Dressed, Future President, Most Popular, and so on for the yearbook, nominees to check, votes to count. My name was nowhere.

I shrugged at him but stopped writing. "What does it look like?"

He asked me again, why wasn't I in the running, for Best Eyes or Most Likely to Succeed, something? He still didn't really know anything about me, for all I wrote and all he read. I didn't know how to write about those things, the doctors and medication and everything.

"You're the prettiest girl here, and you're smarter than any of them." He meant what he'd said, I could tell. I pulled on my cheeks from the inside and held it together.

"Why would they nominate me for something if they don't know if I'll even be here through Christmas?"

I pushed the paper back to him, and then he was in front of me, kneeling, his face right there. His right hand was resting on his khakis, he was wearing a maroon plaid button-up. "And why wouldn't you still be here? Where are you planning on going in the next three weeks?"

I pretended he couldn't see me. I felt swallowed.

I rolled my eyes. I could feel my blood in my body. It was so stupid. I stared hard at the linoleum floor, I heard him get up and walk away. I heard the classroom door shut. I looked up, expecting an empty room. But there he was. Looking right at me.

"Hey," he said. I watched a stupid tear fall on my pants, a small, dark circle appearing.

"Hey. Ali. Here." His face was directly in front of mine now, and I was sure my makeup was everywhere already and

I looked red and ugly and I didn't understand why he hadn't left. My hair a curtain against the swelling tide. And then I felt his hand push my hair away from my face. I took a deep breath.

And I just told him. Everything. About the doctors and my diagnosis, *depression*, *a mood disorder*, *insomnia*, how I wouldn't sleep for days sometimes and I stopped going to class forever and all the meetings and how I just wanted to die, like actually die, and the medications and the therapeutic day school I was at for all of my junior year because I had basically failed out of high school my sophomore year, my mother arguing in meetings with the vice principal, the language of *legally required disability accommodations*, the stares from other students, the rumors, all of it. My arms, the scars. More than I had ever told anyone at once. And he just leaned on one knee in front of me while I choked on air. Like a proposal without the question.

"And now I'm here and it's awful," I finished, furiously trying to wipe my face clear.

I expected the worst, the very worst, his face green with nausea and disgust when I saw it, or fear, that look you give to a crazy person before you walk away. I knew that look. I felt his hand again, but on my knee—I looked up and there he was. I stopped breathing.

"I am so glad you are here," he said. "You're not going anywhere. Not if I can help it." He smiled at me. He meant it. And those words pushed down hard on my heart, heavier than anything that ever came before, a conquering hero to rescue *me*.

Years later, Atwood would echo that moment in me—
*This is the one song everyone would like to learn: the song that is
irresistible.* That was a lesson in how to be irresistible. That
moment in my body when the teacher put his hand on my
knee to comfort me was the understanding of all of that—
that in order to be attractive, irresistible, to be worthy of
notice, was to be both beautiful and in open need, to be dam-
aged. The perfect artistry of pretty and pain. Nabokov wrote
that beauty plus pity is the closest we can get to art. I needed
the teacher's gaze to feel beautiful.

18

I was now in part two of *Lolita*. I thought it was pretty boring. The endless driving, the roads winding on and on, pages of maps and scenery and hotels and motels. *This is romance?* Then, come chapter 13, Dolores (Lolita) is stagestruck. *Oh,* I thought. *She's like me.*

This was the first time I felt like I had something in common with Lolita. While, of course, I had wanted to *be* like her this whole time—the level of desire and power and enchantment she had—I knew I was a poor imitation. Perhaps an improving one, but still—a copy. I watched Lolita through the looking glass of Nabokov's language on the page and was hypnotized. All I wanted was to mimic her in everything, since, really, she was in control the whole time. She got what she wanted. I wanted that too. I wanted to be like Lolita.

Rehearsals for the play were moving along swiftly, with the big weekend of performances staring me in the face. It was my first time having a lead role. I began getting heartburn, acidic anxiety bubbling up from my stomach into my throat. I was trying *so hard* to be good at this.

The teacher told me we needed to talk. No numbers, no notes—he whispered it to me in the auditorium as I was putting my script away after rehearsal. "Tonight," he said, letting his hand linger on the back of my sweater.

The sour taste of my own stomach filled my mouth. I must be doing horribly. I was embarrassing him. I dawdled my way into my coat and out of the building so I was the last one in the parking lot, leaned my arms against the steering wheel, and cried into my dashboard, certain I was going to be replaced. Not just from the play, but there was probably already another girl he was with too, tonight was just a big *Sorry, you're not good enough* talk. At least he wanted to do it privately. I swallowed everything up, fixed my mascara, and went to the diner to wait.

Mr. North walked in while I was stirring sugar into my second coffee "warm-up." He shook off his scarf and coat and ordered a tea for himself with a nod to the waitress. I stared into my cup.

"So," he said as he poured his hot water. "How do you think the play is going?"

I moved my stare to him. "I don't know. How do *you* think the play is going?"

He laughed like he knew a secret.

"You're wonderful, Ali."

"What?" I sputtered.

"I think you're doing great. You've really stepped up. Everyone sees it." He squeezed his lemon wedge into the cup. "Don't you think so?"

I looked at my coffee for answers. "I guess?"

He went on, about how strong my choices were, how rehearsals had a different tone when I was onstage, that Mr. Ulman was truly impressed by me. "You're definitely in the running for the Theater Arts Award this year," he added between sips.

"Oh, wow," I whispered back. I hadn't made it through the school year before, much less been considered for the award, given to the most promising, hardworking student actors in the school.

"But, I think you can be even better." He cocked his head. "Don't you?"

"Um, yes, definitely."

"You know, some of the best are Method actors. You know what Method acting is, right?"

A bell rang far away in my mind. "Totally."

"I mean you could be the next Marilyn Monroe, Angelina Jolie. You've seen *Gia*, right?"

I had. Angelina Jolie was gorgeous and had a lot of sex in that movie. Mostly with other women. I had seen it more than once.

"So, you know people are getting suspicious, and that can't happen. No one can know how I feel about you. That would ruin everything." He reached his hand across the table to mine. "You like spending time with me, right?"

I held my breath as his hand lay on top of mine. "Yes."

I knew there were rumors. It seemed like things had quieted about me for a while, that I was integrated more and more, especially with the play, and I was no longer an interesting source of gossip. I laughed with other students onstage. My old friend from elementary school, Richie, was in the show with me. We had done a theater summer camp together, and he was always kind and warm. I never overheard my name when I walked by him, unless it was a "Heeeeeeeey, Alisson!" calling my attention to tell a joke or talk about a musical. He was popular, on the football team, too, so his acceptance rippled. Things were feeling calm again.

But people had noticed the attention Mr. North gave me in the auditorium. Another girl in the play commented how I was "always hanging around him" as she smacked chewing gum on the steps outside during a break in rehearsal. She didn't have any lines. "Are you guys like, a thing?"

"Um, *no*, like, ew. He's so old." I rolled my eyes for effect.

"Uh-huh," she said, blowing a bubble. I *ugh*ed with as much attitude as I could summon. Her pink bubble popped.

—

I had told Mr. North about that the next night, and he put his head into his hands, pushing his dark hair away from his face. He didn't say anything for a while. When the waitress came over with the coffee carafe, I shook my head.

"Don't you understand what you've done?" His face was still down, but his voice told me everything.

"What did I do?" I hadn't done anything—I told her *no*, we were definitely *not* a thing. Why was this my fault?

"I've got to go." He shoved on his coat and the napkins into my water glass.

"What? Hey—"

"Ali. I am risking everything for you. *Everything.*" He walked out, leaving me the check.

—

That was the week before. I still went to his study halls, but he didn't write. I stood by his desk, eyes big, but he just said, "Yes, Miss Wood?"

The first time it happened I stormed out and ran into the bathroom, slamming the doors behind me and crying in a pale pink stall. The next time I just sat down in the classroom and drew stars in the sawdust on my desk. Stared out the window. Read my script. Then in rehearsal, he called me over to do a line reading and asked me if I had any cravings, maybe for fries? And here we were.

He then explained how we needed to create *plausible deniability*, that otherwise he couldn't see me at all anymore, it was just too risky. Did I want him to lose his job?

"No, no, you know I'd never do anything—" He held his hand up to me.

"I know. So I need you to start dating someone," he said, stirring his coffee. "Not for real, of course, but just to distract from us. Like Method acting. Practice makes perfect, you know?"

"Right."

"You know I'm dating someone."

I knew. He would talk about her sometimes, how pretty she was, how great the sex was. She was blond. I didn't know her name. "You have to understand, Ali, this isn't real yet.

I have needs," he explained. "I mean, there's another seven months until . . ."

In seven months I would graduate high school. We hadn't ever said *it* yet. But I knew—we were going to be together. We just had to wait until then. Obviously. And I was totally cool with that.

"You want me to be miserable that whole time?" he asked. I assured him I did not, that I understood. But it was an ache I nursed, something I couldn't even write about, knowing he'd read it. I had to be cool. Definitely not needy. Anything but needy.

He finished his tea and told me to bring a list of possible guys I could start dating to his study hall tomorrow, that he'd help me the whole time I dated the guy, direct me even.

"I really want to see your commitment to this role, Ali." He patted the table as he got up. "Show me what you can do."

I stared at the paper place mat under my coffee cup and saucer, began writing out my lines from the script. I already knew who I could start dating. David, the boy in my creative writing class who I went to the School of Visual Arts with, was best friends with this guy, John. John was a little older and should have been in college but wasn't. I never found out exactly why. I met him when I was hanging out with David on a weekend, just driving around, getting endless Dunkin' Donuts iced coffees, even in winter. John started joining us. Sometimes before they'd drop me off, John would ask me if I wanted an iced coffee the next day, even if I had rehearsal. And so he'd meet me on the front stairs of Hunt to deliver it the following afternoon, plastic coffee cup full of ice, freezing his hand in the cold wind. The blueberry iced coffee was my favorite. He always remembered. John liked me.

I thought John was cute. He had dark hair, was tall and very similar to David: kind, a stoner, funny. I always had a good time with them, it never felt weird or judgy. John had tried to kiss me a few weeks earlier when he was dropping me off at my house one night, Incubus playing on the car radio. They were his favorite band. I liked that "Wish You Were Here" song. I turned my head away from him and smiled *good night*, knowing I was doing the right thing since my heart belonged to someone else.

That night in the diner, I realized the teacher was *so* right, it was *way* too obvious. *Duh*, I said to myself and my empty coffee cup. Why didn't I see this coming?

19

Almost immediately, I had a boyfriend. John kissed me simply, leaning over the stick shift of his car on a weeknight, not too late, home before curfew. My mom approved, she had met him for the first time the night before.

"He's nice," she said as I pushed along the cart in the grocery store. She was considering bags of pasta. "He's sweet. How old is he again?"

—

Almost as immediately, I knew dating John was a mistake. John really liked me. Like, *really* liked me. I could tell. He was soft with me in a way that felt safe, like the beginning of maybe-love, that period where you aren't sure if anything is real so you don't think about anything too hard. He never pushed his body on mine, he just wanted to hold my hand. He liked to look at me, even though I kept my clothes on. He laughed easily and thought it was cool that I wanted to be an actress or maybe an artist, and when I told him about my previous years of failing high school and wanting to die, he just hugged me really hard and I realized he was maybe going to cry.

And he wasn't who I wanted at all.

I don't think I can do this, I wrote to the teacher in his study hall.

Mr. North didn't lift his head, just pushed back the paper. *Don't you want us to be together?*

YES! I underlined the word. *But I feel bad.* I drew an unhappy face.

I'd feel bad if I lost you, he wrote. Another unhappy face. This one with a tear.

I rolled my eyes at him. "Seriously," I mouthed back.

No one can find out about us. It's too risky right now. If it's a secret, we're safe. This is all on you, Ali. Whatever you want makes me happy. If you want to date another kid, you should. Or don't, whatever. I just want you to be happy.

YOU make me happy, I wrote back.

Then show me what a great actress you are.

I will.

Prove it. I need to know you take this—US—seriously. You have to promise.

OK!!! PROMISE.

"Good," he said, smiling at me. "Better get to class." He scribbled a hall pass, his hand touched mine for a second.

I gave a little wave to Mr. North and readjusted my backpack. But the way John looked at me haunted me. It made me feel mean in a way I didn't like. I wanted to talk about it all to someone, but I knew I couldn't. Who would it even be? I was getting along well enough with the other students in the play, some of my classmates even, and there was always Mrs. Miller. I shook my head as I walked down the empty hall. I had to keep my promise. *Secrets are safe.*

20

The week the play opened, the teacher asked me if I wanted to get married. I nearly spit out my Snapple.

His English class was discussing *The Great Gatsby* that day, which I'd already read. *Bor-ing.* He dropped the note with me on his way to the front of the room, starting a lecture.

I stared at the paper, him back at the chalkboard. *It's happening.* Imaginary white dresses and red roses and candles overwhelmed me, but I forced myself to breathe. *Play it cool, Alisson.*

I wrote back, *Who's asking?* Coy but inviting. Perfect. I folded the paper back over, pushed it to the middle of his desk.

I spun a sterling ring around my finger, wondering what it could be like to have a diamond one. I didn't own any real jewelry, everything was from Contempo Casuals or Claire's. I imagined it would be like those flashes of magic in stories, a prince puts a ring on a girl's finger and *bam*, she's radiant.

She's a princess. Or she becomes a powerful sorceress or something. I just knew it would be transformative, even in the real world.

It was like he was talking forever. About the color green, written on the board and now circled. I was *dying*, waiting for him to come back to his desk. At last, he told his students to read silently for the rest of class.

He sat down, unfolded the note. Smiled, wrote something, pushed his dark hair away from his face. There were only seconds left until the bell rang, and he slowly, so slowly, pushed the paper to the edge of the desk within my reach.

The bell rang as I snatched it off the desk. The dim roar of chairs moving and bags opening around me. "I've got a lot of work to do tonight, Miss Wood. I'll definitely need to get some tea later, after rehearsal."

I unwrapped the paper and read—*Just wondering. Is that a yes?*

Yes, I wrote back. *You?*

He scribbled back: *Depends on the girl. Loyalty is important.*

I wanted to rip the paper into shreds, throw the pieces at him like spurned confetti. I was dating John *for him*, it was literally his idea. Instead I folded it back. "Huh," I replied out loud.

"I need that back," he said as he pulled at the paper in my hands. His voice, now lower, "Secrets and all."

"Yeah," I said, letting go. "Well, gotta get to art class."

"You want a pass?"

"No, thanks, I'm good." I knew he was watching me. I tried to walk sexy, with a wiggle, like Jessica Rabbit. I tossed my hair as I passed through the threshold of his door. The second bell, ringing through me.

—

I ignored him the best I could throughout rehearsal. Which was actually impossible, since he was telling me what to do sometimes. After we wrapped, late, I saw him look at me while I was packing up but didn't go to him like I normally would. I left without saying goodbye, maybe for the first time ever. I was sick of him playing with me. *This is just a game to him*, I thought, slamming my car door behind me, spinning the volume knob up up up on a Fiona Apple CD. And then I was in the diner parking lot.

Without even meaning to, I had driven to our diner on autopilot. I scrunched my face into my hands, I wanted to scream, but instead got my bag from the passenger seat and sat down at our booth. Ordered a coffee and french fries. Opened my journal. And wrote, knowing he would read it, if not tonight, then the next day or the day after:

Dec. 3rd

Today I was asked on the question of marriage.

I've never been asked so plainly, so unabashedly, before. I was asked, and I said yes . . . I am just unsure as to whom at this time. It made me ponder. . . .

I began aimlessly drawing on the place mat and heard the bell of the door. There he was, walking toward me. Mr. North.
I knew he would come.

21

I know the play went well, I wrote it down in my journal: *I know the lines, I know the blocking, I will be great just like I should be.* But I don't actually remember very much. This is what I do remember:

Closing night. Before the show, everyone was taking pictures with their disposable cameras, swarms of orange and black plastic boxes in the room. I had left the flowers John had brought for me opening night on the counter where I put on my makeup, stiff plastic wrapped around pink carnations watching me get ready. Another girl was trying to French braid my hair, but it wasn't staying. A surplus of bobby pins, I was in makeup and costume already. Mr. North came up. "Hey, Miss Wood. Smile," he said as another boy took my camera from my hands. The specific revolve of clicks as the boy readied the camera. I bit my lips, tried to make them seem fuller, trying to place my face in the sexiest, most come-hither, Lolita-esque pose I could—big eyes, red mouth, full of desire. I looked right at the teacher through the flash.

—

Intermission. It started to snow. I went outside in my costume—a summer blue-and-white dress, bare legs—and right toward the teacher, who was standing on a corner, smoking. I thought it was so cool that he smoked. We were alone outside at the edge of the parking lot, huge windows facing us from the theater arts room, which served as our dressing room, and I knew other students had only to look to see us.

I felt like a snow queen, I wasn't even cold, like something was protecting me from the elements. I wanted to kiss him. He saw me coming. He opened his arms and gave me a hug and almost a kiss on the cheek. "Keep breaking legs," he said into my hair. I looked up at him from inside his arms and tried to tell him *Kiss me just kiss me please kiss me* through slow blinks, and instead he squeezed me harder and let go. I stood there for a moment in the snow, taking one last breath of his smoke, and walked back to our dressing room. I had the lead part in the school play after being gone the year before, assumed dead or crazy. I was spending hours after school with other students, working together, building something on a stage. I memorized lines, practiced, laughed, played theater games, stayed late. I know those things happened. And I don't remember any of it—just the parts with him.

22

I thought I was a poet. I had already been writing for years before I met Mr. North, more than a dozen journals packed with words, all these feelings I tried to understand by placing them in front of me, by separating them from myself. As a girl, I had a diary with a lock on it. As a teenager, I hid my journals in my dresser.

I had dated other poets before. My very first real boyfriend, my freshman year, would write me poems, handwritten on pieces of paper I would tape to my wall alongside all the other things that mattered in my life. It was *very* romantic. It made me feel special in a way I couldn't speak, the very idea that someone thought enough about me that he had to write it down so others could understand it. These feelings someone else had about *me*. It was all breathless and red roses and cheeks.

I wrote poems all the time. I wanted to be the next Sylvia Plath, eating men like air and lyrically boasting about it on the page. But writing is a lonely art. There is no band to join, company to dance with on a stage, chorus to sing along with. You sit and write, only you and your pen. So when Mr. North had mentioned he was going to start a poetry club at the school back in September, my heart bloomed like a flower. And now it was finally happening, just as the play ended. Another reason to see him every day.

It was basically a slam poetry team. There were four of us, including this one girl, Sarah, a sophomore, who had won some fancy poetry prize the previous summer, and it was really her idea with another English teacher that started the whole thing. She seemed nice enough but knew she was talented and made sure you knew it too. At our "practices," or meetings after school, we'd have some time to write and then try reading it aloud in front of each other. Since it was slam, it was a lot about the performance. Mr. North arranged for us to compete against another high school at the end of January, so there was pressure to be good enough to not embarrass ourselves. Good enough to maybe even win.

We were getting ahead of ourselves. We needed to practice, and practice in front of an audience. So even though the team was small, the room was usually full of other students who came to watch, mostly girls. There were always girls around Mr. North at school.

There was the one girl from the play, Christina, who hung around a lot. I hated her. In the way that teenage girls are set against each other, competing over something ephemeral and unreal, usually attention from a guy. While I beat her for the lead part, she got a smaller role and somehow always had a question that only the assistant director, Mr. North, could answer. The night of the cast party, as she hugged him good-bye, I saw her give him a kiss on the cheek in the darkness of the doorway. She turned and saw me watching, and smiled.

It was humiliating, but I asked him about her, under the fluorescent. He told me it was nothing, there was no one he cared about like me. If anything, it was a good thing, because it lowered the suspicion on *us*, he explained. So I made sure the next day, when I knew Mr. Edwards would be moni-toring the hall, to lean against the lockers and look up at him, to laugh and play with my hair as we talked. Mr. Edwards was another young English teacher whose classroom happened to be across the hall from Mr. North's. The bell rang, and I asked Mr. Edwards for a pass, which I got. I waltzed by Mr. North's open door and open mouth to my next class, floating the pass in my hand behind me.

It worked. Too well. Mr. North was furious and stood me up twice in a row. I found myself writing, *I'm sorry about Edwards—he truly does mean nothing, he's nice.* . . . *Part of me was curious to your reaction, and now I know and I won't do it again*, pushing my open notebook to him in his study hall. Mouthing, "Please." I was forgiven.

But now, at the slam team, there was also Sarah, the girl who helped start it and was supposedly so talented. She was *all over him*. And he just let her flirt with him, openly. I couldn't stand it. He was always telling me to back off, not make it obvious, *secrets are safe*, but then let Sarah just sit next to him and bat her eyes? *Whatever.*

One day it was especially egregious. I saw him write something in her notebook and her laugh in response. The way he smiled and watched her mouth—I had seen that look before.

I left without a word to him and avoided him for the next day. Went to all my regular classes on time, present and accounted for, even my assigned lunch period. We had a slam practice the following afternoon, though, and I wasn't going to let him ruin it for me. I meandered in the hallways, trying not to be early. Mr. North was waiting by his door and saw me turn the corner.

"Miss Wood?" he called.

I tightened my teeth together.

"I need to talk to you about something," he continued. I walked slowly to him and was suddenly in a group of the other members of the team and a few other students who wanted to see what it was all about, everyone excited and early to practice. I walked in the middle of the pack to Mr. North's classroom. I sat in the back and tried to keep my face toward the window when I wasn't talking to someone else or practicing. Near the end, when we were supposed to be freewriting, getting down starts for new poems, he slid a folded piece of paper under my journal.

You seem aloof today. Seems as though you are mad at something. Is everything all right? Please be honest. I didn't see you yesterday and am concerned a bit. Any help?

I looked up at him. He was at the blackboard, facing us, keeping an eye on the big clock above the door. He turned, chalk in one hand, eraser in the other, wrote *10*, and made it disappear. I knew what Mr. North wanted. I knew I would go to the diner that night and wait, order french fries and a Coke and listen to him, to whatever he wanted to say. Yet somehow my mouth was always empty. I went back to my journal.

That night he was there when I arrived. He had already ordered us two teas, french fries. *He* had been waiting for *me*. I sat down across from him. I had already decided I wouldn't talk first, that it was on him to make this better. He looked back at me.

I listened to the glass chatter of plates, mugs, going from hands to tables and back. An inoffensive eighties pop song blowing from the speakers. I folded my hands.

He took a sip of his tea and pushed a folded piece of magazine toward me. It was an old cover of an issue of *Rolling Stone*, from the 1990s, Jimi Hendrix, long dead, against a blue background, addressed to Hunt High School.

"I don't get it."

"Turn it over, Ali."

I turned it over. "Oh."

It was an ad for some expensive fashion brand. A white guy in a black leather jacket, his face and arms and body pressed against an alabaster girl with long brown hair. She was completely naked. From the angle of the photographer, her bare buttocks took up an unequal portion of the page.

I looked up from the image, my face a mix of shock and hope and confusion.

He lowered his cup and voice. "That's how I imagined you after school. When you were practicing your poems. For everybody. But I knew it was really for me."

I knew I was bloodred. My face, neck, and even chest

skin in overdrive, I knew I looked spotted and blotchy at best. I tried to smile back at him.

He had asked me about my underwear lots of times, he had talked about porn, but he had never actually said he imagined me naked before. We talked about desire and connection, how we were star-crossed lovers and had a love no one could understand. But it was just words, script on napkins, numbers in white chalk. It was shapes and circles and things I could trace and understand. Even my boyfriends before had never said anything like that, it was always how much they loved me and wanted to prove it, how they wanted to hold me, not just my hand but go *all the way*. Romance and sweetness. It was then that I realized he was not like my other boyfriends. It was then that I realized I had a lot of growing up to do before I graduated, in only a handful of months, before we could be together. I realized this was something I had never done before.

23

It was almost Christmas. Late at our diner, snow outside, mittens and hats and the whole New England winter thing. He asked me what I wanted from Santa.

"I don't know, a gift certificate to Sam Goody for some CDs?"

He laughed at me. "Let's see if we can do better than that, Miss Wood." He took a blank sheet of paper out from the pile of student essays and began writing: *ALLISSON'S CHRISTMAS LIST.*

"Um, that's not how you spell my name." I examined my spoon carefully.

He dotted one of the L's. He was writing in block letters, not his usual excessive script.

1. Journal

2. Fountain pen

3. Clothes from "Urban"

Urban Outfitters, the really cool store that was only in the city and expensive, but all the college girls shopped there. So I tried to, too, even if I could only afford a T-shirt.

4. An English teacher.

He looked at me and smiled. "Right?"

"Um, maybe?" I tried to be coy, glad I had put lip gloss on before I came in.

He laughed and kept writing.

5. Green paint.

This was a private joke, because green meant longing, like how he explained to me about Daisy's dock, the meaning of that symbol in *The Great Gatsby*. I had missed it before he told me. It was so obvious that I felt stupid, but I rolled my eyes like I already knew.

6. Gift certificates to:

-Rhapsody in Brew

-Anywhere that doesn't sell grandma bras. I don't buy the "sheer" shit.

He had begun starting our nights at the diner together by asking what underwear I was wearing, teasing me to show him my bra straps, telling me that anything other than black lace was for kids.

7. A rose.

8. Something (anything) to replace the fuzzy dice.

He hated the red dice I had hanging from my rearview mirror. I thought they were cute.

"Well, what about what I want?" I said, knowing I was whining.

"Fine. What *do* you want?"

9. Shoes.

10. Red hair dye.

"You want to dye your hair red?"

"Yeah, why not? Brown is so boring." I tugged on my ponytail. I wished I looked like Ariel from *The Little Mermaid* but didn't dare say that aloud. What's grown-up about wanting to be a Disney character?

"No." He crossed it out. "Your hair is so sexy. Don't you dare change it."

"Oh," I said. "Okay then. Well, I want more lip gloss."

11. Lip gloss.

"So what are you going to give me?" I asked him. He looked back at me and laughed.

12. Hershey's Kisses. Eh. Hem.

"Do you think you've been a good enough girl to deserve all this?" he asked, and smiled.

"Uh-huh."

"Well, you just keep dreaming, Ali," he said, and crumpled up the sheet.

"Hey, wait," I said, and grabbed the paper back from him before he could start ripping it up.

"Hey yourself—you don't get to take things home."

"But it's not even really your handwriting, no one would know," I pleaded as I held the fistful of paper close to my chest, my eyes big and asking.

He sat back in the booth and considered me. He leaned in. "Can I trust you?" he asked me, very seriously.

"Oh yes, you know me." I nodded along.

"Pinkie swear?" He held his hand out over the table.

I held my pinkie out and he wrapped his finger around

mine and pulled my whole hand into his and squeezed, whispering, "I trust you, Ali."

I squeezed back. "I trust you too, Nick." Like our hands were kissing, the thing my mouth wanted to do.

24

John said he was sure he loved me. I wrote in my journal, knowing Nick would read it too: *January 2nd. John told me he loved me and it wasn't going to change and he loved me. God it's ringing in my ears. Now what?* I wanted Nick to tell me what to do.

That night when I showed him, Nick wrote back on a piece of notebook paper, tore it out, *Do you ever feel like you could fall in love with me?* The ink was soft on the white, he used his favorite fountain pen, the one he wouldn't let me try. He said I would bend the nib and ruin it with my script because I was left-handed. I kept smoothing the paper out, over and over on the table, as if I could feel the words with my fingers if I pressed hard enough. Like it was an incantation, repeating the question over and over in my mind. Like if I spoke, the spell would break.

I nodded back at him.

"I don't want you to miss anything," he told me. I wanted

him to hold my hand. I thought I was going to cry. He assured me that I should be confident about the summer, that it would be here before we knew it. This was just how it had to be right now.

I nodded again. He told me he had to go do some grading.

He was already getting up. He left me at our booth, $5 on the table. It all made me feel very sad and very stupid. Sad for waiting, stupid for doubting him, us. And maybe stupid for believing him too.

All the same, I kept writing in my notebooks, knowing Nick would read them. *All I think of is N. That's horrible. If only John was a jerk or something, or N told me he didn't want me, or something.*

The next afternoon, I was waiting for John to pick me up. He was taking me to a concert that night. The teacher stood next to me in the corner of the parking lot, smoking. A bunch of girls surrounding us. I saw John's car come up.

"Have fuuuuuuuun," a girl crooned at me. She thought John was cute. I smiled, pulled on my backpack.

"Miss Wood? A word?"

He put his hand on my shoulder, ducked his head near mine, and whispered, "Don't fuck him."

Everything went hot inside me. "Why not?" I snapped.

"Because I'd be jealous."

I couldn't put words together fast enough. The teacher was already walking back to the group of giggling high school girls, cigarette smoke blowing behind him.

I slammed the car door behind me, embraced John across

the gearshift, and kissed him with everything, tongue and hands in his hair. I wanted the teacher to see. I wanted the teacher to feel something about me.

"Well, hello to you," John said softly.

"Let's get something to eat," I said, buckling myself in. As we drove away, I looked back for Nick. He was already looking at me.

25

Nick remembered my birthday. He got me a present more than a week early, lining up with his own birthday. We met in the parking lot in the dark and his skin touched mine while he placed the package in my hand.

1/4/02 for 1/13/02

Alisson;

One fountain pen writing to give another. I hope the ink flows from your soul as well through this as it does from a Bic. May it doodle many stars and assist in making certain that you become one. . . . There is no doubt that it will.

Perhaps one day it will pen the lines that lead to a gold sticker that reads "Pulitzer" or, and more importantly, it will be a gateway to feelings, tears, gritted teeth, silvery smiles, and care. To you I wish a perfect 18th birthday year, brimming with grand imperfection, for that is what makes us real. Fountain pens bleed like we do, skip like we

*do, run out like we do, and can be refilled like we can. The
other things that make us real. Breathe, love, taste life, and
then . . .*

   Write it all down.
   Happy Birthday, Alisson.
   *Another real writer waiting for unreachable stars to
fall into my green heart . . . And writing it down.*

In my eighteen years in the world, I had never read *anything* that romantic. After I read the card under the streetlights, he took it back and told me he'd return it after I
graduated. There was more of my present, too, I just had to
wait. But I got to keep the pen.

26

A week later.

"So what about *my* present?" Nick asked me, stirring his tea.

"What do you mean? You said no presents."

"And I broke the rules." He twisted the string around the tea bag, the dark tea staining the milk like ink. "For you."

I was mortified.

"It's not like I *forgot* your birthday—"

"I know, Ali. I just feel a little silly, going to all that trouble for you." He shrugged as he sipped his tea. "It's no big deal."

I felt like I was shrinking, like Alice at the tea party. Everything was wrong and it was my own fault.

"Well, what do you want?" I wanted to smack myself immediately for asking. Making it so obvious that I didn't know what to get him. I couldn't ever keep my cool around him.

"You know what I want." He was watching his tea.

I felt like an idiot. I had no idea.

"I've been risking it all for you, Ali. You know I could get fired for this?"

"Yes, I know—"

"Well, what exactly are *you* risking, Miss Wood? What's on the line for you?" He pushed his cup away, talking to me like we were back in school.

"Oh my God, Nick, I would never—"

"Yeah, I know, you're not gonna be my pink slip." He took out his wallet and put cash on the table. "But right now you could go to the principal and I'd be fired in a minute." He snapped his fingers for effect. "It's your word against mine."

It was interactions like these that made me think I had power in the relationship, that I wasn't just an eighteen-year-old girl being manipulated by her twenty-seven-year-old teacher. And maybe I did have *some* power, maybe. But I don't know if I would have been believed even if I had gone to the principal or some other adult. After all, Mr. North was right, it was my word against his. What had I ever done to make myself seem like a reliable narrator?

I mumbled about being sorry into my hands, how he was so right. I wanted to hide underneath the booth. The floor looked gross, though.

"I'm risking everything for you, Ali," he said. "I'm baring my fucking *soul* here for you. What have you shown me?"

I twisted my mouth and nodded, trying to learn. Wanting to prove my devotion, somehow.

—

I got home late and sat on the floor of my room, PJ Harvey on my CD player, softly, to not wake Lauren next door. He was *so* right. What was I risking? I needed to show him how much I cared, how much he meant to me, how much I trusted him.

I pulled out a photograph of myself, one an ex-boyfriend had taken of me a year earlier, tucked under my desk calendar. It was from the side, topless, but nothing to see, really, other than the tiniest half smile of the bottom of one of my breasts, covered by my crossed arms. My hair falling in messy waves, looking away from the camera, another half smile on my face. It was taken in his dorm room, one weekend when my parents let me visit. I kept the negatives.

I had a blank canvas on the floor. I began putting things on top of each other, layering the photograph, a pair of fishnet stockings I sacrificed for the cause, silver wire wrapped around the framing. I realized I needed to paint it first. Green. Like longing, like in *The Great Gatsby*. Like the teacher's fountain pen.

The paint dried overnight, and then I glued things on in an artful way in the quiet early light, using glitter spray paint for a final touch. Between the fishnets and wire wrapped around and around, you could barely see me and my body, and even then you could barely see anything. Would it be enough?

I wrapped it in newspaper and a ribbon. I gave it to him in the parking lot of the diner, and when he opened it he glowed.

"Wow," was all he said. I could tell he wanted to kiss me. I wanted him to. Badly. I looked up at him, in longing.

"This is perfect, Ali," he said, opening his arms for me. The hug was quick but overwhelming, we were alone this time, no one watching, his arms were so much bigger than any I was used to, and I could feel his erection against my hip.

Whoa. My breath caught, like I was scared. But an image of a black-and-white movie appeared in my mind, the femme fatale purring, *Is there something in your pocket or are you just happy to see me?* I pushed my jaw into itself. *Grow up*, I said inside.

I kicked snow as I pulled away. "No big deal," I assured him. I had shown him I was capable of creating desire, that I could do this, that I wasn't just some dumb, clueless girl. This was a power I had, too, that I was his equal in all this. The wanting went both ways.

27

The slam competition was at Rhapsody in Brew. The café was packed, standing room only with students from both high schools, because of the popularity of a guy on our team who played football. The other girl, Sarah, read her poem first, the one that won her the prize, and she got a high score. Then we were switching back and forth with the other high school's poets. The football running back from our school went up next for us and read his poem with lots of energy and bravado, got everyone to clap. Another student from the other school followed. Then it was my turn. I was the last performance.

Once the poetry team had officially started, the pace of my poem writing drastically picked up. I wanted to be on the team so bad. I wanted to be a part of something again, now that the play was over. While editing my poems was nothing new, the teacher's notes now took on a more urgent tone: *More of this moment / Why this word?* I made all of his changes, bringing him new versions every time I saw him,

churning out draft after draft of stanzas and lines and feelings. Furtively scribbling lines in my journals, like Humbert
in *Lolita*. I wanted to impress Mr. North at the competition.
I wanted to make him proud of me, of what I was becoming
under his careful hands. I decided I would read a new poem,
one he hadn't seen before.

It was obviously a love poem. "To N." N. could be anyone,
it didn't have to be the teacher, Nick North. Double conso-
nant, like Humbert Humbert in *Lolita*, he pointed out once.
There are lots of N-beginning names. But I was sure it would
be like the numbers on the chalkboard, code just between
Nick and me.

I started reading my poem in front of everyone. There
were phrases I stole from my writings back and forth with
him—"copper and quarters," "like my lipstick," repetition
of the word "hold" in the last stanza—but who could possibly know that? While I had managed to save the occasional
hall pass, the notes from the diner were so much harder to
keep, to hold for longer than the few hours we spent there.
Torn into pieces. Ink and napkins blooming in water glasses.
Folded and put into his pocket. But every so often, into mine.

I finished my poem, one hand holding the mic, the other
reaching into space, dramatic like I wanted to be. The crowd
screamed and clapped like they had for everyone else. I put
the backs of my hands against my cheeks as I sat down, certain I was red. I felt like everyone was staring at me. But for
maybe the first time, in a good way.

It was time for the judges to score me. It was a mix of the
advisers from both schools and audience members chosen at

random, on a scale of 1 to 100, all the way to decimals. The guy from the football team held my hand hard, because my score could mean we won. It was like everything was under ice, that moment before something breaks through.

The judges announced they had made their decisions. They held up pieces of paper with the numbers in marker—one after another. Trying to do the math in my head. The last one and then the full score. The room broke open—not only did we win, I had the highest personal score that day. It seemed like everyone wanted to hug me, my loneliness countered with so many warm bodies all at once. I cried, but hot, happy tears, as even Sarah with the fancy poetry prize squeezed herself around me and shouted into my ear about how awesome I was. I looked for the teacher. I expected his arms at any minute, his eyes to say all the things he wanted, how proud he was, how wonderful I was. But he was talking to the other teachers, laughing and shaking hands. He left without even saying goodbye.

The poetry team—Speakeasy, we had named ourselves—got a write-up in the *Hunt Weekly*, the school paper. Mr. North, as one of the faculty advisers, was asked his opinion about the match. He said we exceeded his expectations. "I was pleasantly surprised," he was quoted.

My stomach filled with bricks as I read it. Exceeded his expectations? I made him proud only because he thought I would suck.

I stomped through the rest of the day, using art class as an excuse to rip up paper, working on the color background for the next assignment. I crumpled things up and smoothed them out, over and over, as an exploration of texture, for the whole period.

Nothing I did was good enough, I knew it. All I did was disappoint him. I swung around wildly inside, between anger and embarrassment, convinced I was the worst for even thinking I had done well at something, *what a narcissist*, and then convinced he was the worst for not being supportive, *he's such a selfish dick*. Writing both sides of this internal narrative in my journal in the same entry, the same page even. Hoping he would read it, eventually. He wasn't reading my journals as regularly anymore. Who knew when he would even know how I felt.

28

A few days after the slam, after my pointed sulking, Nick wrote out the lyrics to a John Mayer song, "Love Soon." He said, that night in the diner, "This is how I feel about *you*. Only you." I mouthed the words as I read the lyrics, all longing and secrets and love. My chest moved slow and heavy and everything was forgotten.

Still, he told me again, this had gone too far. Things were happening, but nothing had *actually* happened. Even though the determined lines had not yet been crossed—a kiss, a phone call, telling—he maintained that it had gone too far. I already knew about the other similar transgressions, Nick had sworn me to secrecy over coffee—how a math teacher was dating a girl on the softball team, but Nick explained that the teacher had gotten permission, that her parents had signed something and it was fine. A secret, but fine.

Nick told me that we couldn't continue like this unless I signed something too. I was eighteen now, he reminded me,

I didn't need my parents' permission. I wasn't sure why the sudden need for formality, I didn't know what shifted inside him to make him so upset. That night he had the contract ready for me; I remember it reading:

> I, *Alisson Wood*, do solemnly swear to not keep anything from our time outside of the classroom or anything not directly related to school. I will give everything written down to Nick North for safekeeping and/or destroying. I hereby swear that anything I write is a lie and completely fabricated. I make things up all the time and am not truthful. You cannot believe anything I say.
>
> *Signed:* _____
>
> *Date: February 7th, 2002*

He told me that unless I signed it we couldn't even talk anymore. That I needed to protect him if I really loved him.

He never said that he loved me, though. And now I do not know how much of his story about the math teacher and another student was true—I didn't know her, had never heard those rumors. But I also cannot say what was or wasn't being said about my own relationship with Mr. North; teen gossip is not a reliable source. Even if it was true, that the math teacher was sleeping with a student, would her parents' "okay" make statutory rape charges disappear? That girl was younger than me, a junior. It was too unreal, even down this rabbit hole of our relationship. I felt like Alice in Wonderland, like everything was mixed up and nothing was familiar, things were the same but nothing made sense. And we were both trapped.

The teacher loved it when I referenced Lewis Carroll. That was my second birthday present, a paperback copy of *Through the Looking-Glass* that he inscribed to me. Nabokov would say that "Lewis Carroll Carroll" (as he called him) was "the first Humbert Humbert." In *Lolita*, Humbert describes the perfect nymphet as having *Alice-in-Wonderland hair*. This was a game the teacher played with me, in how he used Nabokov, Carroll, and Edgar Allan Poe, all to show how ordinary and also special our relationship was, how romantic, how in the tradition of other great writers. Like how Humbert would list name after name of important, intellectual, artistic men who also happened to love young girls as a way to both romanticize and normalize the perverse predilection, both things at once.

But that day, Mr. North handed me a pen. *Don't you love me?* I signed the contract and never saw it again.

Later, it would remind me of Humbert's diary, the words that caused the death of Lolita's mother. How she stumbles upon them and revolts from him, runs out the door screaming that he will never see Lolita again, stamped letters in hand to warn others of Humbert as predator. But then—an accident. She is hit by a car. The letters scatter on the asphalt. Humbert tells us it was all such good luck. A critical reader might consider the narrator—given Humbert's motives, it's fair game to question his reliability in this telling if this was *truly* an accident, since Humbert had everything at stake, everything to lose—his Lolita—if he had been revealed.

There was no such luck in my life. No one stumbled upon my journals, or his. No one walked into the diner late at night and asked what a student was doing in a booth with her teacher. Our contract was never discovered. But I wonder: What would have happened if it had been found?

29

Only weeks later we were fighting in his study hall, in the shop classroom, machine tools and sawdust everywhere, snow falling on the other side of the windows. There were only a few students in that period, all freshmen, none who knew me except as *that girl who's always around Mr. North.*

We fought on paper. I ripped his arguments in front of him and balled them up into the trash can. I glared, shut tight as a seashell, refused to write back. I swung my backpack on and nearly growled out loud and marched out, passless, into the empty hallway midperiod. Halfway down the hall I heard him—"Miss Wood! *I did not dismiss you!*"

By now, he called me that only when he was mad. Or when he was making a show of the student-teacher power dynamic in front of some other teacher. Either way, it was for an effect.

Another student turned the corner, saw me. I felt like molten and rock in the hall. I locked eyes with the student, who looked instantly sympathetic when he heard Mr. North yell; in that way, all students are alike—no one wants to be yelled at by their teacher.

I made Mr. North walk all the way down the hall to me and glared as he hissed why I *cannot do this to him right now* and *can't we just talk about this later.* He was upset about my boyfriend. The boyfriend I had had for two months now, as explicitly directed by Mr. North. I was doing exactly what I was told, so I didn't understand the sudden problem he had with John.

The night before, at the diner, I told him about a date John and I had gone on, seeing a movie and walking around after, then driving with the radio on and how he held my hand, and Nick started scribbling on the place mat immediately and wouldn't show me what it said. He gulped the last of his tea and balled up the paper, dunking it in the water glass as he walked out of the diner without saying goodbye. I pulled it out and tried to flatten it, but I lost most of the words to wet paper tears. I could still make out the words "as if," "little slut," and "love." I dripped more water onto the wet place mat, the waitress gone the whole time. It was like I was the only one in the diner, like I was all alone.

The next day I got to school on time, determined to ignore Mr. North for the rest of the school year, because he was just a jerk who didn't understand anything and had never made me a single real, true promise or given me anything to hold on to. Just words on pages he destroyed, and I was sure that Ms. Croix would start tutoring me after school if I just asked, I didn't need him for anything. After all, I had a boy-

friend, someone who *actually* cared about me. Like I needed
the teacher. I would never speak to him again.

—

By fifth period, I was in Mr. North's study hall, big eyes
and apologies. I held our notebook to my chest and whisper-
swore I still hadn't slept with John and I was *so sorry*. How I
didn't care about that guy at all and it was just stupid. I wrote
all of it down on yellow lined paper and folded it and passed
it to him. I stood there while he read it. He took out his green
pen and wrote back, *Ok, but are you going to break up with
him?* As Humbert swore in *Lolita*, he did his best to *tackle the
problem of boys.*

I twisted my face. *No,* I wrote back, *you haven't broken
up with that blonde.* Knowing about her was one thing, but
she had come to school one afternoon the week before and he
kissed her in front of me in his classroom. I ran out into the
woods next to the senior parking lot and pushed my mouth
hard into my hands. The next night at the diner he had told
me, *Alisson, she means nothing. But adults need to be in adult
relationships. You won't be an adult for another six months. . . .*

In study hall, he started writing angrily back, *absolutely
forbidden,* and I wrote angrily back again, *whatever,* and then
he wrote, *harlot,* and I just stopped reading entirely. And
then I rushed out.

Now, in the hallway, he was whisper-yelling at me, he
reminded me of the contract I signed and how this had to
stay between us, and eventually I just nodded and promised
to listen later. I could only play with power in school, whereas

he could send me to the principal's office. In school, I was whoever Mr. North said I was.

He led me back to his study hall and I did not read or write or stare back at him. I looked at the parking lot outside the windows, the thin light of winter afternoon, my car in the senior parking lot corner, how I had gotten my spot that day, how I was early. I waited for the safety of the bell and walked out. Said nothing. But later that night I walked into our diner, sat at the corner table, ordered tea with lemon, and waited until late, when he showed up, late. And I listened to him explain things to me again.

30

He told me we needed to take a break. This was after he had stood me up repeatedly at the diner, and he never read those entries of my journal, the ones where I filled page after page, waiting for him. He didn't actually say it, he wrote it. A piece of beige scrap paper from the shop room, *Can't, maybe next week, not right now.* I got the message.

He was still dating the blonde. I had broken up with John. I couldn't take it anymore, the guilt. Even though I wasn't seeing the teacher as often as I used to, even though it just wasn't the same now, I knew I couldn't love John like he wanted. Things felt empty all over.

I still went to Mr. North's study hall, but now I just sat quietly, writing less and less. Outside, things melted and grew. But I felt stunted.

It was like a darkening, a quiet return. But now I had friends, kind of. People I could go to Friendly's with, drink endless coffees with, laugh with. No one close enough to trust with such a big secret. Sometimes other students would comment on how much time I spent with the teacher, but beyond *Oh yeah, he's tooooooootally cute* and blushing at his name, I said nothing. Girls would ask if we were "a thing," and I demurred. *I wish! If only! In my dreams!*

Privately, I felt abandoned by him. Weeks went by without a real conversation. I barely wrote in my journals. What was the point? It all felt stupid.

It went on like this for months. And then—spring. Everything changed.

One day, his study hall. The smell of sawdust. He was trying to coax me into writing back, mentioning coffee, disco fries, but I was tired of being stood up and told him so. I was *so* over all of it. We were using my tiny notebook, the kind that waitresses might use, the kind that almost fits in your hand.

He tore out a page and wrote:

No matter how wrong I have ever thought all of this was . . . no matter how we got on each other's nerves at times . . . (and even when you're not in the greatest mood) those eyes smile at me. I hear your mind, I scare myself at ever doing or being or thinking it or (ghast) knowing it but when your eyes and your mind say what your lips have already said I know that
I
LOVE
YOU.

REALLY.
OOPS.

Pushed the page to me. Waited. Watched.

I had told him that I loved him only once, in the winter, in the middle of all of it happening, late at night standing in between our cars in the parking lot of the diner, and immediately regretted it, wished I could erase it from the air. He just smiled at me and said good night. I knew I had lost the upper hand, with my dumb, teenage, mushy declaration of love.

That was weeks, months before. And he remembered! And he loved me too! He saw my love for him even through my irritation and exasperation. It was like the seasons changing around us, things buried only to come back.

I wanted to shove my face into his own right there, never mind all the other students. I wanted him to kiss me like I saw in movies, like when you're dancing and he dips you deeply, further into the kiss. But I knew how to play this game now.

I looked up at him. Met his eyes. Mouthed back, slowly, "Yeah."

He took the paper back from my hand and crumpled it up, threw it into the trash, the bell was ringing somehow already and I had to go. He wrote me a hall pass without me even asking, I knew this was all happening again, that he had never stopped caring, it had all been an illusion to keep us safe. Knowing he was right there, I reached into the trash and pulled out the crumpled page. His hall pass in one hand, the ball of paper in the other, I drifted off in the direction of whatever class I had next, it didn't really matter. I knew he was watching me. I looked behind me, smiled back. We looked at each other. And I was so certain. This was true love.

31

In the end I had choices. To the shock of everyone, especially me, I got into multiple colleges: Bennington, Ithaca College, a state school, and Manhattanville. Despite my uneven transcript, I was wanted.

Manhattanville offered me the most in scholarship money and was the closest to NYC. In the end, I hadn't applied anywhere in the city, all those schools seemed too advanced and out of reach. Manhattanville was the next-door best thing. It seemed small, close enough to home in case I had to deal with any emotional or psychological troubles again and needed my mom. It felt safe.

Bennington was the school I had wanted. It had no grades, no majors; students were encouraged to create their own academic and creative path and received only written evaluations from their professors. It was a tiny school up in Vermont, full of artists and creative types. It seemed like somewhere that would push me and also watch me close enough that I would be taken care of. It seemed like somewhere I would be seen. And supported. I didn't know what I wanted to study—everything? I felt like all I had done was lose my time in high school to medications, depression, trying to get better. I didn't want to keep losing things.

Nick knew that Ithaca College was the right choice for me. It was a midsize traditional college, with a strong liberal arts school. It had a well-respected theater program and was one of the only colleges to offer creative writing as a major, not just a minor, for undergraduates. And it was in Ithaca. Where he'd be in another year. Where he told me we could be together. He had played another show the weekend before, told me the night before that the second song would be for me, a cover: John Mayer's "Love Soon." *He played our song.* I swooned.

We had never kissed, but I knew what I wanted. I checked the box, *accept offer of admission*, and mailed my choice to Ithaca.

3 2

I wasn't a virgin. He knew that. He made me write about all those things already. A precocious child, a willing teacher. But now I was eighteen. And all too willing.

He already knew about my high school boyfriends, high school heartbreaks, high school firsts. He told me he was glad, jealous but glad, because if he was my first, it wouldn't be right. Humbert's *unwillingness to morally corrupt a child*, after all. But Dolores Haze, his little Lo, Lolita, she was not a child. She confessed her previous copulatory entanglements with a boy, slightly older from summer camp, to Humbert, while I confessed my previous copulatory entanglements with boys, all slightly older from my high school, to Mr. North. No, I boasted. Exaggerated. I let my words balloon on the page because I wanted so badly to be seen as a *woman*, as someone worthy of attraction. I wanted Mr. North, Nick, to want me.

And I didn't understand why we had to wait, anyway;

once I turned eighteen, *I didn't understand*—he already knew I could keep secrets. I wasn't going to rat him out, get him fired. I would never do that, and he knew it.

"Not until you graduate, Dinah," he said—he began to call me that, Dinah, the cat from *Alice's Adventures in Wonderland*, in the last weeks of school. Alice's pet. Another favorite book of his.

We both knew what was coming, and it made me dizzy. But I felt lucky too. He thought I was sexy. It wasn't the same as with past crushes. They had been only a few years older, no one ever older than nineteen. I worried I wasn't prepared for the discrepancies between an adolescent boy and a man's body. But I had tried to ready myself.

I got my first bikini wax. I don't know why, there was barely anything to remove, but I convinced myself that the pain was a punishment for everything that happened there before Nick North, that the beeswax and muslin was my penance. I tried to pay attention when he talked about religion. I knew he would marry me only if I took the sacrament, ate the body and drank the blood. He wanted to marry a Catholic girl, a good girl. I was none of those things. I tried, and it didn't stick. I knew he was disappointed.

I considered the burn of the molten wax as my own sacrament of sorts. I couldn't lock myself in a tower and call for him, I couldn't poison myself with fruit for him to find. But I could get a Brazilian wax. And I was proud of myself for keeping quiet through the whole thing. I didn't scream or even yelp. I wasn't a child.

Before that, I had ordered lingerie online, with my father's credit card again (now I wonder: What did he think I was buying?), paying extra for expedited shipping to be sure it arrived by the time I graduated. The Victoria's Secret pink-and-black tissue paper–filled box arrived two days before the ceremony, and I tried on my purchase before my parents returned from work, Lauren at tennis practice. I was alone in the house. I ripped open the clear plastic that packaged each item. I had picked a baby-blue sheer bra, thong, and skirt set, with soft mesh and black satin ribbons on the edges of everything. I put it on, piece by slippery piece. Tiny rows of hooks and things to tie. I stared at myself in the mirror. It didn't look right. The sheer fabric somehow both exposed and hid at once, mostly exposed. I hated my body. The stretch marks on my breasts and hips had finally begun to fade, now more like lavender, but you could see the scars on my arms, tiny light lines from over a year ago, but still. There.

I had never let a boy look at my body in the light. Never. Lights were always off in their rooms, it was always night-time in the back seat of cars past curfew. As if it weren't really happening if they couldn't see my skin. But I knew I couldn't stay hidden this time—Nick had already seen lots of women, probably, and he wrote over and over about how he couldn't wait to see me "in something sexy." I thought he'd like this. And the skirt would hide my hips, maybe he'd even leave it on the whole time so he'd never see me, really.

But there, in the distilled sun of my hallway, I looked like a child in an inappropriate costume. I wasn't wearing enough makeup, that was it. I painted myself in my darkest colors, shuffled the roots of my hair with my hands, pursed my lips at my reflection. It wasn't working. I looked even younger. I just looked stupid. All of this was stupid. I smeared my mouth with my hands and stomped barefoot to the bathroom sink, my careful lines washing away. All at once it sank into me: *This might actually happen now, he won't want me because I'm a child, I haven't even gone to college, he's probably slept with tons of beautiful women, I'll make a fool of myself, I don't know anything, I'm just some crazy girl, he'll laugh at me like this, he'll just see a little girl in a stupid outfit, how could I ever have thought a man like that would love me.* All of those thoughts filled my head and had nowhere to go.

I rubbed my eyes—my fingers were black with mascara and eyeliner. I heard a car pull into the driveway. My mom. I ran into my room and changed my clothes back to a tank top and shorts, black cotton undies with something flirtatious written on them in bright pink on the backside. I heard my name, I yelled that I was *upstairs*. I put the lingerie back in the plastic bag, tucking it under the mattress of my twin bed.

33

It was already decided—once I graduated, we would be together. *For real.* I was seeing Nick most nights again, passing notes in classes, even in the hallway. It felt like with the end of school in the air, everything was freer somehow.

Prom was the only thing I did without Nick. But I didn't want to go. I had been to all the school dances already in my years at Hunt, and even though I had friends now, thanks to the teacher's collusion to weave me back into the social fabric of school, I still felt like an outsider. I didn't trust anyone. I still hadn't told a soul about my future relationship with Nick.

"I don't want you to miss anything," he said again and again. Prom was important, a major milestone, something to remember fondly for the rest of my life.

So I asked a boy in my science class, Sean. I had known him since middle school. I got a dress. Blue satin, halter neck, with pockets. I loved the pockets. I bought matching shoes.

Coordinated our flowers. Got my hair done at a salon. My nails too. Got a tan the week before since I was so pale and Sean was darker, Lauren imploring that I would look like a ghost next to him without one. She went tanning with me. The sickly smell of coconut and burning all over mingling with warm air in the car as I drove us home.

Sean picked me up wearing a rented tux. He had borrowed his mother's car, which was nicer than his. No limo for us. He brought me a matching corsage for my wrist. We took pictures in front of my fireplace. My mother *ooh*ed and my sister told me we looked cute together. I made a face. It wasn't like that. Sean seemed to be as neutral about prom as I was. I had had to ask him after all.

Then at the park across town, more photos with big groups of other seniors in the rose garden. Posed for the formal shots once we arrived at the hotel ballroom. Him behind me, arm around my waist, his damp hand on mine. *Smile!*

We danced all night under colored lights. There was a disco ball. If my shoes had been glass, they would have shattered. I had fun. We ate the rubber chicken and drank endless sodas and laughed with our friends, some of whom I had known for close to ten years. There were moments I forgot who I had been, what I was carrying, and if you watched me from the wall, you would see a normal teenage girl enjoying her prom. Like everyone else. Spinning in a boy's arms.

That night there was no looming deadline. I would not turn into a pumpkin at midnight, there was no curse limiting me. The prom ended with a slow dance, swaying to Boyz II

Men's "It's So Hard to Say Goodbye to Yesterday" in Sean's eighteen-year-old arms.

Sean was someone I felt safe with. We'd been in classes together for years, and aside from two days in the eighth grade, we'd never dated. And then, "dating" was staying on the phone for hours after school as you watched TV together, clicking in other girls or boys from our class using three-way calling. When he "broke up" with me later that week, I slammed down the phone on the receiver so hard it rang a little, a final note of sadness.

By the following week, I was going steady with his best friend, who gave me his silver ID bracelet to wear, which made it very serious. It was middle school, after all. And Sean and I were back to being friends again. Sometimes on the phone, sometimes meeting at another neighborhood boy's house to play video games or burn CDs from Napster. He wasn't someone I thought about having a crush on. Sean never tried to flirt with me, and I didn't flirt with him. He wasn't someone I wanted.

Throughout the night of prom I found myself constantly scanning the room, looking for Nick. Was he chaperoning? He hadn't given me a clear answer. I hadn't seen him all night.

Sean and I walked back to his mother's car, not an enchanted carriage, and then I saw Nick on the outskirts of the parking lot, smoking a cigarette. I don't know if he just came at the end or had been there the whole time. I knew he saw me. I wanted to go to him, but Sean tugged at my arm—we had to go home and change, then go to the post-prom event, an all-night parent-organized carnival to give us something to do other than drive drunk and have sex. There was no chance of Sean and me having sex. I looked at Nick as we drove away, at one point swinging closer so I was sure he could make out my face in the open window, and I wondered how much he saw, what he thought of me.

Even though I had gone, and had fun, all of it, as Sean drove us home under the stars, I wished I were with the teacher instead.

34

He wrote in my senior yearbook, taking up two full pages, more than any of my friends:

June 26th, 2002

Well, it's been a great year for you. Figuring yourself out artistically and best of all: trusting, loving and believing in yourself. Now, you are off to college in upstate New York (and a great one at that) and you are so ready to go . . . so mature. . . .

I respect your drive, admire your determination and am in awe of your talents. Please don't waste any of that and never get down on yourself no matter how bad things seem. They will get better. I thank you for trusting me with your writing, some of which was very personal and required a high level of trust. I thank you for your smile and bright face (especially when it was in school on time) . . . it sometimes lifted me up enough to finish my day. I hope

I've provided an insight or two in your life that weren't there before. Overall, I hope I have helped at some point this year.

May you have the best of luck at college. I know you will be fine. I hope to see you soon. It was a great pleasure to know you better this year. I, for one, will miss your enthusiasm and energy in school. If you need anything, just find me here. Good luck.

His signature, a flourish, green ink and longing.

35

There are photos of me on the day of my high school graduation, tan (which for me isn't very tan at all but left over from prom preparations) against the white cap and gown, big smiles with my little blond sister. It was hot, June, a big metal stage set up on the end zone of the football stadium. Four hundred or so graduating seniors that year on the bleachers, everyone's name read aloud one by one by one in the cloudless afternoon, sometimes with booms of applause and the release of balloons, usually the same monotonous clapping. More photos with my family or friends from elementary school whose parents had fond memories so they squeezed us together in a frame; dozens of photographs and the same smile. I am sure that there were big hugs between me and Mrs. Miller, Ms. Croix, Mr. Ulman, Mr. Edwards, even Dr. Williams. I'm sure my father shook their hands and my mother said things like, "How about our Ali." Somehow, I had ended up graduating with honors. I received a small scholarship for my upcoming fall in college. I don't remember any of those moments, though I can hold the photos in my hand.

I remember the teacher coming up to me and giving me a big hug, squeezing hard, how he smelled like sandalwood and salt, and whispering into my ear, *Call me tonight*, as he pushed a tiny piece of paper into my hand. I still have it, the paper with his phone number, in a box within a box.

I don't have a picture of the two of us. Not one, not together. Later he will take pictures of me in my underwear, of me in the car, in the woods. There will be rolls of film with a photo of me, then a photo of him, then another of me; there will be sequence, a timeline of images, my face looking back at him. All I could think about that day in the white cap and gown was how much I wanted that time, my time with the teacher, to start. It was all I wanted. Even though I didn't know what that would mean.

36

The night after I graduated, I went to his apartment, a half hour away. I wore a dress, the baby-blue lingerie underneath. It was uncomfortable, I kept tugging at the edges of the underwear the whole car ride. "Why are guys so into thongs anyway?" I asked no one.

Nick's place was on the water, the smell of the ocean flooding in the night air. I had to cross a wooden walkway to get to his door, the wood was gray and too soft to give me a splinter. It was like walking across a plank, the sound of the waves in the background. I breathed in time with the tide.

I knew exactly what was going to happen: he would answer the door before I finished knocking, a John Mayer song on in the background, and spin me around as he brought me inside. He would bring me close into this arms and there it would be: true love's kiss. There would be candles, we would make love gently, and he would tell me he loved me and mean it. And I would fall asleep in his arms in a house without someone's parents, without anyone to find us. I lied to my parents about where I was going. I was ready for this.

And this is what happened: I knocked on his door and waited. Instead of spinning me into a deep kiss, he pulled me inside, hissing, "Someone might see you," John Mayer on the stereo, a scented candle that cloyed. I stood in the middle of his living room and rubbed my knees together, my skin smooth because I had just shaved my legs and put on fancy lotion—Juniper Breeze by Bath & Body Works.

He asked me what I wanted to drink. I'd only had sips of warm beer foam at parties without chaperones or under someone's porch, the smell of stale beer forever linked with dirt and pine. He was waiting. I was disappointing him already. An image of Sarah Jessica Parker with a pink martini glass was suddenly in my mind. I didn't watch *Sex and the City* because I was too embarrassed that my parents would walk in during a sexy part and I would die, just die, but I saw the ads. "A cosmo," I said, like I knew what I wanted.

I sat on his brown couch and looked around the room. Wrought-iron café table in the kitchen, a bookshelf against the wall with glass doors, which I would later learn held antique books. Framed Alphonse Mucha prints, oil-painted girls with pale skin, long, liquid hair, jewel tones advertising cigarettes.

He laughed at my face after my first sip, reassured me that it would get better the more I drank. So I did that, tried to keep up with him and his pineapple gimlets, Humbert's drink in *Lolita*, he reminded me. I still hadn't really read the whole book. He told me he was drinking it on purpose, in honor of me and him and us. That would be one of the last clear sentences, before the cosmopolitans overlapped and overwhelmed me, his drink in his hand, tapping it against the edge of my martini glass. "To us," he said, and told me to take another sip. He kept making me cosmos, and then somehow my clothes came off, my fancy lingerie making up for my fear. He didn't seem impressed by my purchase from Victoria's Secret. Somewhere between the drinks I lost how it all began, I lost our first kiss.

He asked me if I wanted to go to his bedroom. I told him I would be there in a minute and went into the bathroom. I sat on the edge of the bathtub, cold tile on my bare feet (*where did my shoes go?*) and most of my bottom, and tried not to vomit. The cold shocked me into sharpness. This was not going at all how it was supposed to, this was not a night of romance. Obviously, it was all my fault. I opened the window above the bathtub, letting in the salt night. I could still fix this. I stared at myself in sheer blue lingerie in the mirror.

I knew what to expect; he had told me, made me tell him months before. He had written it in that note in his classroom, he'd passed it to me across his desk, how big his penis was, *Can you handle this?* I took big gulps of night air.

I walked into his room and he was sitting in bed, hairy chest, half under the covers. He was writing something in a notebook but saw me and put the pen down. Almost a year later, I would take that piece of paper and everything else from the drawer where I knew he kept all of our letters and physical proof this happened and leave my key on his bedside table, the last time I would be in his apartment. The sheet of notebook paper, lines about *longing* and *waiting for our forever*, how my lingerie was a present and he *couldn't wait to see what the pretty wrapping contains.*

I had never been in a full-size bed with someone before. This wasn't the same at all—the boys I had slept with before were scrawny, just the same soft, bare skin, and always asking if I was okay, if it hurt, *are you sure, are you okay?* Always in the dark, always in a moment, in a corner in the basement of their stepmother's house. They were boys, I was a girl. Their hands would hold mine tightly and tell me how much they loved me as they apologized for how quickly it all came and went. They never crushed me.

With the teacher, sex was different. It was blurry, all a haze, he tugged at me, I made noises like it hurt because it did, but he didn't ask what they meant so he didn't know. I let him hurt me. I had such bravado before, I had told him I knew what I was doing. But now I was drunk. I had never been drunk like this before. I spun. I went rag doll and he pushed my legs farther apart. And then it was over. He was sweaty on top of me, he kissed my cheek and my neck, his hand in my hair. He rolled off of me, left one hand on my bare breast, told me he loved me. Then he snored. I lay next to him, awake for a long time. Even though I was still, the room rocked. I didn't know where my underwear went. I didn't know that that night was everything our relationship

would be, wouldn't be. I didn't understand what had happened, I thought it was going to be completely different. I
had wanted it so badly for so long.

I had to accept the fact: this, in all its difference from my
fantasy, this was what I wanted.

part ii

capture

If this were a fairy tale, my story would be over. Not only had I found my prince, the teacher, but he rescued me, saved me from myself and my loneliness. Over my senior year, I had proved myself special, worthy of his care. I, now eighteen, was worth the risk he took (losing his job) to love me. Under the hand of a different author, maybe Lewis Carroll, the Brothers Grimm, or even Nabokov, this would be the part where there is a beautiful description of nature or light to wrap things up, a slow fade into darkness, the darkness being understood to be a metaphor. (For what? A world overwhelmed by love for a man? A love so strong it blocks out all other light?) This should be my happily ever after.

Looking back, I realize it is easy to see this is where the narrative breaks down. This is the part in my story where, as an adult, I can see how a schoolgirl's everyday unrequited crush transformed into something much darker, much more dangerous. This is the part where things begin to go wrong in ways that I, as a girl, could not anticipate. This is the part of the story that, even almost twenty years later, I hate to tell. There is no fairy tale here.

1

I woke up alone in the teacher's bed. This was the first time I saw his room in the daytime. His cat, black, fluffy, fitting her name of Duchess, was in a ball on his pillow. How had I not noticed her before? I smelled coffee. But I smelled something else too—maple syrup? Was the teacher making me breakfast?

The cat glared as I sat up. I had never woken up naked. Anywhere. Ever. I had seen this happen on television, and the girl always wrapped herself in the sheet, Ariel in *The Little Mermaid*. I began to tug at the white top sheet, which disturbed Her Majesty and she gave a low growl. But I was successful in my costume. I dragged the sheet behind me as I checked my makeup in his bathroom mirror (a mess, I was full raccoon, so I smeared on more concealer and lip gloss), ran my fingers through my hair, brushed my teeth. Tousled yet still fuckable was the look I was going for. Easy. Effortless. I wake up this beautiful every day, I could confirm. This is just me. Every day I—

The teacher opened the bathroom door into me.

"Hi." I tried to bat my eyes at him. The train of my sheet dress was clumped between the back of the door and the cabinet. "How'd you sleep?" I tried to purr and reach the hand that wasn't holding the sheet around my chest out to him, and he met my hand midway.

I realized too late, it wasn't in kindness.

"What the hell did you do to the sheets?" he said, squeezing my hand enough that it hurt. I looked down at my improvised dress.

"I didn't know where all my clothes were and—"

"Not this sheet"—he pulled me back into his bedroom—"this one!" And he pointed to the bed.

He let go and I shuffled closer to the bed. A smear of black mascara in two areas, approximately the distance between my eyes, defiled the white pillowcase. But worse, the pure white fitted sheet, approximately halfway between my head and feet, had a small but deep red stain. *Fuck.*

"Oh," was all I could muster as I rewrapped the clean sheet around me tighter and began to hoist the long end into my arm and muddle toward the mistake. "I can fix it, I just need some soap and cold water and—"

He grabbed me again.

"You said you weren't a virgin, *Alisson.*"

"I'm not, I told you about—"

"Then why did you *bleed*?" He pulled me close, but not like last night. This was not a time for rejoicing, this was not ancient Greece, when vestal virgins were celebrated and Hestia worshipped for their presumed virginity, this was a wholly different scene.

Years later, I will be able to articulate that pain during sex has nothing to do with sexual inexperience—it's about your partner being too rough. I bled after sex with the teacher because I was a child. I was barely 110 pounds, I had been only with other teen boys, all of us children. I was eighteen, but that didn't matter; for all intents and purposes I was still pubescent. The teacher was definitely not. There was no fear, no gentleness, on Nick's part; he wasn't careful in the ways I was used to. Before, sex was brimming with fear—of being caught, of causing pain, both emotional and physical, of consequences, fear of regret. My body was simply not prepared for the force, for the aggression, of sex with a grown-up. At eighteen, I didn't understand my body. I was ashamed of it. I didn't realize that it was doing exactly as it should have, looked exactly as it should have, that I was perfectly acceptable exactly as I was. At eighteen, I understood none of those things.

In the moment, I tried to explain it somehow, my only understanding then that bleeding a little just happens sometimes after sex and it just hurts a little and I'm sorry and, and—but he only got angrier. He shoved Duchess off and stripped the bed of its white. I stood in the middle of his room, my eyes open but watching his wrath as if I were mute from a spell, but I promised him I was still honest, even in a bedsheet, I promised him I didn't lie, that I was definitely, distinctly, repeatedly, *not* a virgin, all of which was true, he read it himself in my journals, but he was still mad.

Waving the white sheet like a flag, the teacher began yelling about Charlie the rapist, not Humbert the therapist, and how he wasn't supposed to be my first lover, you brat, as I just stood there, and I knew he was yelling something about *Lolita*, but I couldn't place it quickly enough. *He's yelling about* Lolita *now?*

What I didn't remember: this was the scene when Humbert first rapes Dolores, Lolita. It is after he picks her up from summer camp, they have been crossing the country in a seemingly romantic road trip, it is after Humbert realizes she had been with another boy that summer, another camper named Charlie. Dolores is coy, playful about her fling with Charlie when retelling it to Humbert, even offering to show him what she learned. She doesn't yet know her mother is dead. She doesn't yet know that this road trip has no destination except endless motel rooms and beds. Humbert is furious when he learns Dolores has been sexually involved with someone else, and his jealousy erupts (as it usually does) in wordplay. In his mind Charlie, a boy similar to her age who "defiles" her, is the rapist; yet he, Humbert, who is now her legal guardian, who drugs and rapes her in a hotel, is not a rapist but a *the*rapist. Because fucking is a way of fixing things, of making it all better.

The teacher was fixated on me *not* being a virgin—it would have been wrong if he "deflowered me," he said. But since I was decidedly not a virgin, what would he be taking? We spoke of my sexuality like it was a thing to be tossed back and forth between hands like an apple. From his view, bites had already been taken. Having the first taste would have been wrong, but the fruit was already rotting. What was the harm in him just taking another bite of me?

He kept on about *Lolita*. He threw the pillowcase with my mascara smears into the sink and blasted the hot water, began to do the same with the bottom sheet in the tub, and I realized he didn't know what to do with blood, I was the expert here.

"Wait, no, it will only set the stain—"

He turned to me; I now fully noticed his own clothing, a pair of navy boxer shorts, a white T-shirt, and I had never seen him in this light before, of morning or rage.

"What?"

I tried again to explain how hot water makes blood stain fabric and you need to use cold, and his face collapsed with his legs onto the bathroom floor together, his face in his hands. I had seen this in movies. He was so quiet, it was only the hot water screaming from both taps. I stepped over him and turned off the hot water in the tub and switched it to cold, tugged the ruined area directly under the water.

"See? It's already getting lighter," I assured him with a confidence I replicated from years of my mother and laundry, of already having period blood staining my underwear or pajamas by accident more than once. "It's going to be fine, sweetie." I shook the wet sheet with my hands close against the stream.

I didn't know what made him snap, my presumed knowledge of how this worked or the use of *sweetie*, but he did. He began to yell. At me. So much so that I tried to back away and stumbled over my sheet dress and the porcelain and into the tub, all the sheets were cold and wet now and I was half soaked in seconds, but I was fine, I grabbed the soap dish on the wall so it was not like I hit my head at all, and he was yelling about how his parents were going to kill him and it was all my fault.

His parents?

He stormed out of the tiny bathroom, water still pouring into the tub, leaving me to soak. I heard a door slam. And then only the water. I counted my breaths. I counted to ten. Heard nothing more than the plumbing. I turned off the tub faucet first. I left both sheets to swim, the two of them blocked the drain so there was a solid inch of cold water collected. I wrapped myself in a bath towel, not white. I remained without my clothes. I turned off the sink.

His *parents* would kill him?

I hadn't heard another door. He was not in the living room. But my clothes were. I blotted the rest of myself dry with the towel, very carefully between my legs, confirming that it wasn't a surprise menstruation cycle, and put on last night's outfit. I still didn't know what the maple smell was. I pulled out another pair of underwear from my bag. I was just tugging them on when he walked back inside.

My hands full of lace, I said, "Um . . . should I go?"

His face was still red. But it was recognizable. His hair was a mess. He looked so tired.

"Hey?" I tried again, now upright. He was still not talking, so I walked toward him and held out my hands again. "I'm really sorry. I'm so sorry. I'll fix it, I promise. I don't think it's going to stain, I don't."

Silence. My hands were empty.

"Um, why are your parents going to kill you? Does, like, your mom still do your laundry?" Trying to make a joke. He was nearly thirty. That could not be right. But it was worse.

"It's their sheets," he explained to me, how this was not actually *his* waterside condo, but his parents'. We had sex in his parents' bed last night. They moved to Florida and left him the condo. So while it was his place, totally, he said, he couldn't just trash things, and they're *luxury* sheets and he couldn't just throw fifty bucks away on sheets every time we fuck and you've got to figure something out, Alisson, this is ridiculous, what kind of sex were you having, anyway? He made a reference to the size of his penis, that it must be so much bigger than the others to cause me to bleed.

"Yes, of course, duh"—I leaned into him, just seeking to stop the anger—"that's it," and nuzzled his arm. I fluttered my eyelashes at him and apologized and apologized until apologies became kisses and we had sex again right there in his parents' living room, and it hurt the whole time, so much I made noises, but I didn't say stop, so later I would tell myself it was my fault he didn't stop. And then when it was over there was blood again. I didn't want to ask him to be gentle because I didn't want him to think I was a child who didn't know what was good for her. I assumed he was teaching me all the things I should have already known about sex, about my body, about a man's body. Without any context for what sex was supposed to be in a real-world way, I assumed this— what was happening with the teacher, the pain, the lying about pain—was just what sex was meant to be like, that it was fine because this time he put the towel under me. And then, as he made pancakes, I in one of his T-shirts and pairs of boxers, he made me list the others and rank those three penises in size in relation to his own, with his coming up first.

So, I assure you, dear reader, he didn't deflower me at all.

2

That summer he told me I couldn't write anymore. I noted it in my journal, *Friday morning, June 28th, I'm not allowed to write. He said I couldn't, no way, no how.*

"It's too risky, Ali," he told me, how he would have to keep everything from now on at his place, in case my parents found it.

He told me this in the morning, his green eyes catching the sun. I had never seen them so close in school. They were flecked with gold and all the variations of green I could imagine. Green like longing. He pushed my hair away from my ears, his voice a near whisper even though we were alone in his apartment. A habit from when he would say things in the hallways, in classrooms, the way his timbre always got when he would say something important to me. Something private.

But now I laughed out loud at him—I shot up in bed, the momentum of my opening jaw pushing past his hand. I couldn't stop laughing. It was just so ridiculous. Now that I was officially a graduate, officially eighteen, why would my parents suddenly start to look at my journals? At anything about my life?

He didn't find it funny.

He got out of bed and yanked on boxers, the band snapping onto his soft, furry belly. I thought his belly was sweet, strangely vulnerable.

"You don't get it!" he yelled to the wall, his back to me. "Can't you for a second think about anyone else? This isn't a fucking joke."

I couldn't remember the last time I had laughed so much I cried, but I called out to him to come back to bed. I reached out, knowing my hair was falling onto my shoulders, barely covering my breasts, I knew he liked when I looked like that.

It didn't work. He pulled his hands through his hair and left, I heard him banging things in the next room. I put on one of his T-shirts and slipped on underwear and padded out to him, barefoot.

I listened to him explain: New rules. We had to be even more careful now. Before, if we were seen somewhere, there was always the excuse of "helping me with a monologue" or "editing a poem," and now we had no reason to be together. Except for the obvious. A teacher fucking his student hours after she graduated could still get him fired. "Keeping it quiet keeps it ours," he finished. I nodded along, sipping coffee from his mug.

But even so, the next morning, before he woke up, I pulled my journal from my backpack and wrote those lines,

I'm not allowed to write. I was so wrapped up in my fantasy, the newness, watching the sky through the window as I sat on his bed, still not believing all of this was happening to me and how could I be so lucky. I wrote a final line in the notebook, *I do hope all goes well. I do wish he was awake,* still hoping that he would read it someday. I wanted our literary love story, the one I was promised that year in school.

3

I thought things would get easier after I graduated. Through-out the year before, over and over in my journals I marked time until we could be together—months into weeks into days—and in my mind I thought we could walk hand in hand under the sun that summer, get ice cream and sit in the gazebo a few blocks from my house, that he could meet my parents as my boyfriend. *She was worth the wait*, he'd say, beaming at me. I thought my world would open up with his love.

It wasn't like that. Somehow my world got smaller. That last page in that summer journal I wrote, *He makes me so happy, the only bad thing about it all is that no one no one can know . . . I have to lie a lot. Where I am. Who I'm with. But it's worth it. . . . Keeping it quiet keeps it ours. I just hate lying.* The rest of the journal stayed blank. I followed his rules.

Since we weren't seeing each other every day anymore,

and since my parents paid for my landline while I still lived on the second floor of my childhood home and could, theoretically, see who called me, Nick and I could communicate only via AOL Instant Messenger. He was Ichabod77 and I was Alissonwondrland. We'd try to make plans and go back and forth over chat about the details—how many miles away we had to go to get a coffee without worrying that someone would see us, which movie theater was not in my hometown but not in one of the adjacent towns where all the teenagers liked to go. We went to see the new *Star Wars* and made out the whole time, like teenagers in love. He made me buy my own popcorn, though, meet him in the theater a few rows apart. He moved next to me only in the darkness of the fantasy in front of us.

Our first movie date turned into a fight, since he wouldn't take me back to his place in his car—I was to wait for him to leave the theater, dawdle, then leave at least ten minutes later and meet him. I pouted and snarled in the dark as the movie ended. I had assumed he'd change his mind. "Someone might see us," he said. He gave my shoulder a pinch as he walked away. That night, I raised my voice back at him for the first time.

The amount of secret keeping and microplanning quickly became unsustainable. So it was decided: we needed to go away. Home and near home were all too risky. The only way we could be safe, where he could truly show me how much he loved me, openly, was if we were far away from anyone who could possibly know anything about us.

He read to me from the book in his bed, Nabokov's lines, the opening of *Lolita*'s part two: *It was then that began our extensive travels all over* . . . I understood how romantic this all would be. How much like *Lolita* this really was.

4

He always drove. The map on my knees that I could never fold right, ever. But there was a destination in mind, under his finger, circled in green ink: Ithaca, New York, a college-and-Nabokov tour bound together.

Cornell, also in Ithaca, was "the same university where Vladimir Nabokov had been a professor," Nick explained patiently, "where he was a famous lepidopterist."

I assumed it meant something dirty, and I tried to play ingenue.

"A butterfly collector," he defined.

"Oh," I said, disappointed. Who cares about butterflies?

In just a few months I was going to Ithaca College, the other side of town from Cornell. But for now, we both lived in our parents' homes. So that summer it felt like all we did was drive.

The drive from his place to Ithaca was nearly half a day. But first I had to get to his place, a half hour from home, park around the block, ring his doorbell. I was late, like almost always, and he was annoyed—"I was waiting by the door, you know." The coming and going, the in-between, that was the real risk when someone could see me. But I knew once my bags were in his back seat and the radio was on and his hand was on my leg he would forget about that. I'd get to choose the CD and hold my hand into the open-window air. I imagined how we could walk together with his arm around me. I loved it, every step.

—

It was hot that summer, and even though his car had A/C, unlike mine, he kept the windows down, my long hair tangled around my face and my skirt blowing up so he could see my underwear, my legs in the fractured rays of sunlight. He wore a baseball hat with a short brim as he steered because he didn't like wearing sunglasses.

I always wore short shorts and skirts because I knew he liked my naked legs. He would fawn when we were alone: *You're so sexy, your skin is so soft, how did I get so lucky?* Uncomplicated compliments that were novel from a grown man, that felt weighted with knowledge. I knew they meant something because he could compare me to past girlfriends, to other legs. With my past boyfriends, there was always an element of wonder and amazement that they never seemed to shake, like they couldn't believe *it* (touching a girl, another warm human body actually next to them) was finally happening; so their compliments were like a shard of glass in the sand—they shimmered, fragments, worthless. Nick had already told me

about his other girlfriends, about how good the sex was with
that girl he had dated during college. I wondered if he compared us in his mind. I wondered what her legs looked like.

—

To drive up to Ithaca we took interstate after interstate until
we eventually ended up on these tiny roads that still claimed
to be interstates, Route 17 northbound for miles. Once we
were upstate, we were the only car you could see, and we
drove between rocks, where the pavement was cut from boul-
ders, all shades of gray. Everything else was green, green,
green, the trees and cut grass and his fountain pen. I brought
the one he gave me, green too.

Halfway through the drive we stopped at a diner on the
side of the road for coffee. The Roscoe Diner. It became ours
in all the ways that counted—the pink neon in the ceiling,
unlimited refills on coffee, the menu that was always the
same, you didn't have to read it to know what to order, so
much like "our" diner back home—but different in the important way: no one knew us here.

Nick held my hand across the Formica while we waited
for french fries. By the end of the summer the waitresses
would begin to recognize us. They were the only ones who
acknowledged our relationship that summer; we stayed at
a hotel once, twice at most, and I couldn't tell anyone, no
matter how in love I was. And I didn't.

That first night we were at the diner during the dinner
rush; we couldn't leave until late afternoon after I got back
from the day camp where I was a counselor to fourth graders.

He wanted to make it to the hotel before it got too late and I was tired. I ordered tomato soup and he got a grilled cheese and we shared. He put on a fake British accent and made his half of the sandwich talk to me across the table, telling me I was so pretty and delicious looking, and would I go on a date with him, Mr. Earl of Cheese Sandwich? And Nick got cheese in his scruff from all this and I somehow got tomato soup on my nose and we used napkins to clean each other up.

When the waitress came by, we were still laughing, and she said, "Stay in love, you two," as she circled the number on our check. And I looked at Nick, my breath caught and eyes wide. In awe and fear: *Someone saw us*. But Nick just held my hand harder. In Ithaca, that summer, we were safe.

5

That summer I pretended I had finished the book, but really I just skimmed it. Once Dolores ran off mid–part two, I lost interest. Skipped entire pages. I was already bored from the endless road trip, the scenery. All the tension drained out of the story once they got together. What was I reading for anymore?

Nick continued to bring *Lolita* up, and I just nodded along, not that differently from when I *had* kept up with the book. He underscored all the important parts—how romantic it was, the Sisyphean task Humbert undertook to ignore Lolita's charms before they could finally consummate their relationship, how Lolita was in control the whole time. Over late-night coffees at the diner back home, the one public place where we could talk, he would take the book from my hands and hold it, the cover levitating over our plate of fries, as he read lines aloud.

When we were at our home diner, it felt like I was still in

high school, like he was still Mr. North. I would take notes on the napkins, sometimes drawing stars if I disconnected from his voice, but I knew they weren't for keeps. I longed for a leather-bound notebook, ink, another tattoo. I had gotten a star on my right hip the day after I turned eighteen, pulling the side of my pants low to show him after school. He gaped. I wanted something permanent, to mark what was happening in a way that couldn't be erased. Everything I wrote he would still destroy.

—

That summer was full of presents. It seemed like every time I saw him was a celebration of me, of us. There were always drinks. There were always boxes tied with bakery string, sometimes with candy or a pair of panties he thought I would like, or lip gloss or grown-up perfume. He said I shouldn't smell like a schoolgirl anymore.

One night, he sat me on his couch and gave me a thin package. Wrapped in newsprint, red-and-white bakery string.

"What's this?" The gift was light like paper.

"Open it."

I untied the string, peeled back the tape. It was a book, almost. A brown folder, half the size of a piece of notebook paper.

"Open it *the right way*." I had had it upside down.

"Oh!" It had a title. *Revised Evidence: Vladimir Nabokov's Collection of Inscriptions, Annotations, Corrections, and Butterfly Descriptions.* It was a book of stamps. He must have remembered from some late-night conversation how I had collected stamps as a child. This was a special edition, surely expensive. The stamps captured butterflies, black-and-white photographs of the author himself, a whole page of different covers of *Lolita*.

I hugged it against my chest, thanking him with a kiss, his cat sleeping on the other side of the couch.

"I knew you'd love it," he said, smiling at me, inches away from my mouth.

"Of course." I kissed him again. "You know I love the book as much as you."

"You're my Lolita," he said.

6

I can't remember the lies I told my mother, but I know I told them. I imagine they were the normal teen evasions: *I'm sleeping over with my girlfriend; I'm going out with so-and-so; Mom, I'm just heading across town, I'll be back later.* I can't explain how I was away for whole weekends. No one could have possibly reached me. Cell phones were strictly for emergencies only, bulky bricks of plastic left in my car glove box in case of an accident. Phone calls were charged by the minute, and my car was always left behind in Nick's parking lot. Somehow, I never slipped. There were never consequences for not checking in, being late, not coming home at all. And the innate danger of the situation I locked myself in never came up in conversation, because I had no one to talk to about it. No one worried about me.

I was away with Nick at least a half-dozen weekends that summer, leaving the safety of my hometown and childhood bedroom to go somewhere else—Nick's apartment, a hotel room, Ithaca. A whole new world, where I wanted to be.

In some versions of the myth of Persephone, she is not kidnapped. She goes to the underworld willingly, she becomes the wife of Pluto without any force. In others, she is stolen away, her cries echoing through Eleusis. In every version, her mother, Demeter, searches for her, unstoppable until her daughter is returned whole.

I do not know what my mother knew that summer. I don't know what she suspected, if she ever wondered, if she ever saw through my lies. Even now, when I ask, she evades—*I don't remember. It was so long ago. I don't remember, Ali.* There is no answer here.

This myth is not a story of a father's grief over the loss of his daughter. Zeus is tangential and becomes involved only when his wife's grief can no longer be ignored. That summer, my parents were on their way to getting divorced but were still living together—part of the reason being that my father wasn't particularly active in our lives. A lot was unspoken in our home. He may remember this differently. I have never asked him if he suspected anything that year, because how could he—he was never the one I needed to lie to. He simply never asked. He was never the river to cross when I left home. That was my mother.

Persephone is described as a beautiful maiden picking flowers the day Pluto takes her from the sun and into the underworld. Her archetype captures innocence in a woman, a girl trapped in between child and adult. I am not suggesting

I was a virgin plucking flowers from a meadow the day the teacher found me. But I was in that ephemeral in-between, that space and moment of wanting both and not knowing when to let go of either. *Can't I have it all?*

In the end, Persephone spends part of the year with her husband, part with her mother. Everyone seems happy. But this fairy-tale ending occurs only because her mother forced Zeus to return her daughter—she stilled the world in endless winter until Persephone came back to her. Back then, I was grateful to be ghostlike in my own home, left to come and go as I pleased. I don't think my mother realized I was missing. Now, I think we both wish she did.

7

I thought he was going to marry me. He told me one night in a hotel that he already knew how he was going to propose, how it would be here in Ithaca, in a gorge, surrounded by green and water. He took me to Tiffany's in New York City on the hottest day of that summer, July, I don't know the exact date because I had stopped keeping track. I had stopped writing, like he wanted.

I had never been to Tiffany's. I'd only seen the Audrey Hepburn movie and imagined myself as the life of a party in a black cocktail dress and diamonds. Months later, in the fall, he would send me the collection of stories by Truman Capote and I would go on about how much better the novella was than the movie. But I always had a soft spot for the orange Hollywood cat. Now, because of Nick, I was finally able to see the glittering storefront instead of just imagining it or seeing it on-screen.

He drove us into the city even though we could have just

taken the train. "Someone could see us," he said. As if I didn't know. I didn't need a reason. I was just happy to not hide.

We went to the store on Fifth Avenue, the big one. My cheeks and shoulders pink from walking in the sun on the sidewalks. Tiffany's both was and wasn't what I expected. It was full of so many people and so many beautiful things, and I had never been inside a fancy jewelry store before, the kind with real armed guards in dark suits and not just mall cops. But it seemed less sophisticated with so many tourists walking through, and any novelty I wanted to experience was mostly overcome with the smell of strangers' sweat.

But still. I was suddenly aware of how wet my mouth was. Nick held my hand as he led me directly to a counter, pointed at something under the glass, a thick, rounded silver band, something that sparkled inlaid in the middle. He asked to see it, if I could try it on, and I just knew it—it was happening, he was proposing right in the middle of the afternoon in front of all these strangers, who would clap in congratulations and not fire him, and I reached out my left hand to the salesgirl across the clear glass, and then—Nick smacked my hand away, laughing.

"No, no, not that one," he said, and grabbed my right hand for the clerk, yanking me. The woman smiled at me with her mouth, but not her eyes. I was startled by the coy violence, and I didn't understand what I had done wrong.

She took my hot right hand and talked smoothly to Nick as she slipped the silver band on my ring finger, describing the carat of the tiny diamond, and then lightly turned my hand like a doorknob, allowing the light to catch the chip of gemstone in the piece. The diamond lay smoothly against the silver; when I ran the pad of my thumb over the cold metal, it barely registered the shift in texture. It wasn't an engagement ring after all.

I immediately felt myself get even hotter, redder. From everything, from the entire situation, from my misreading of it all. I started feeling like I couldn't breathe, like gym class in winter. Nick kept talking to the jewelry clerk, kept holding my hand with the tiny diamond. I was starting to see flashes of light and was maybe going to faint. Then Nick suddenly in my ear, asking, "Do you like it?" as he cupped my chin.

"Yes, of course, I love it," I said, leaning into him and letting my lungs out. He put his left arm around me—he was tall enough that when he did that the top of my head would not even clear his shoulder—and held my right hand in his as he led us to the checkout. Although, in a place as fancy as Tiffany's, you don't call them checkouts, I'm sure.

"We're engaged to be engaged," he said, and squeezed me again. We were surrounded by that distinct Tiffany blue. And I can't help thinking of that exact shade as being a very *young* color, like Easter eggs and the eyes of blond children and high school boyfriends who say things like "engaged to be engaged."

Even after all of it, all of us, was over and burned away, I kept the Tiffany blue box. And the ring. Since it wasn't an engagement ring, I didn't have to give it back at the end.

8

Another trip to Ithaca, weeks later. We were sitting on the steps of some building on Cornell's campus eating grocery store sushi (Wegmans sushi, he clarified, which was definitely not the same as other grocery store sushi) when I realized that in all of the weekends away to Ithaca, we had not set a single foot on the Ithaca College campus, the campus where I would be in just a few weeks.

"Ithaca is our home," Nick told me more than once. "It's where Nabokov wrote *Lolita*, and it's where we get to write our own story."

Years later, I will note how in all of his dramatic readings to me, he never read the foreword when the reader learns Lolita, Dolores, dies. Of course, not that. But back then, he read with such grandeur and enthusiasm that I found myself clapping after each chapter. I didn't notice the omission.

There, anywhere in Ithaca, we could openly be affectionate, and at first it was like a sugarcoating to anything that

caused hurt: the sex, his words sometimes, the secrecy of everything. The salt of pain made everything that followed taste
good. He showed me around Cornell again and again, *this
was where I took comp lit and read Washington Irving, this was
where I read Dickens, this is my fraternity,* where he showed off
that he still knew the handshake with some confused under-
grad who happened to be staying in the frat house over the
summer. Nick walked the halls of Cornell's academic build-
ings the same way he did his old fraternity—with wide arms
and a bellowing voice, pointing with his hands, *this is mine.*
Even though it had been years ago, it was still his. Like how
I would always be his, he would say.

9

"You don't understand intimacy," Nick told me. It was a mid-summer weekend; we were in bed in the morning. My hair was a mess, we had just had sex, I had to pee. I didn't want to have this conversation again.

I sighed into the pillow. This was about doors. He didn't like that I locked the door in the bathroom. This was the tone he took when he thought I was stupid.

"How am I supposed to love you if we don't share everything?" he insisted.

I didn't understand how me having some privacy made him not love me. I started to say this and he cut me off— "How would you know anything?"

I threw the pillow at him as I got out of bed, moaning at him to shut up. I knew *lots* of things! I started to slam the bathroom door behind me and he was there and pushed it open.

"Go *away!*" I shoved the back of the door with both hands and arms and it was no use. He pushed himself into the bathroom. I glared at him like I had never glared at him before. I counted to ten and clenched.

"I would like some privacy, please."

"No." He leaned back against the shut door. He locked it. "We can't have any secrets."

Why is me using the bathroom a secret?

"That's not how adult relationships work, Alisson. How am I supposed to trust you when you leave in a few weeks if you can't even pee in front of me?"

My legs were crossed as I sat on the toilet, seat down, a cold chair, but my face was on fire, I could tell I was red without even turning to the mirror. Oh my *God* oh my *God*.

"Isn't watching me shower enough? I thought you liked that."

He shook his head.

"Please leave. I would like some privacy."

He shook again. He was leaning against the closed door, his arms crossed. "Not until you pee in front of me."

I stared at him, neither of us bending. Then I made a break for the door, I tried to get past him, and it was pointless, he picked me up as I kicked him and screamed at him to let me *go*. He yelled back at me to *shut up* and pulled off the boxers of his I wore to sleep and then I was bottomless and he sat me on the toilet. Seat now up. He held me down by my shoulders and threw the boxers into the bathtub. I wanted to spit at him, but I couldn't unclench anything to open my mouth.

"There—" He gave my shoulders a shove. "I waited before, I'll wait now."

I buried my face in my hands and hair. I could tell from the heat on my skin that my face was blotchy and I didn't know where my ponytail tie had gone. I held it together as long as I could. At first, I talked to myself while we were in silence: *I can sit here forever. I am a marble statue on porcelain. He has no power over me.*

And then, eventually, nature overcame even the angriest of willpower and I gave in. The sound of me peeing in front of him was louder than it ever had been when I was alone. I didn't understand this romance. He handed me back the boxers and kissed the top of my head.

"No more secrets, Alisson."

10

"Let's watch *Lolita*."

"What?" I had suggested the day before that we watch *The Craft*, which he had never seen and I had loved. I had even rented it at Blockbuster before I drove to his apartment.

"Yeah. You haven't seen it yet, right?"

I knew it was a trap. He had told me to watch the movie version that spring, before we were together, as a stopgap in seduction since he still couldn't touch me then. I had gone to the store and wandered until I found Stanley Kubrick's black-and-white classic. I came face-to-face with Sue Lyon, as Lolita, in red heart-shaped sunglasses, sucking on a lollipop, on the cover of the box. I rented it, but I never actually watched it. I just paid the late fee a week later.

Years later I will notice that Lolita is never described as wearing heart-shaped sunglasses, that it was "dark glasses," in Nabokov's words, and Kubrick gave Sue Lyon oval sunglasses only as a prop. But the Kubrick movie poster sprang eternal in our collective mind, and red heart-shaped glasses were weighted with scandal and sex from then on.

"Which version?" I volleyed back. I knew there was the newer one, with Jeremy Irons and Melanie Griffith. My mother had watched it on Showtime, it was deemed too risqué for an American theatrical release at first, and mentioned she thought it was good. I was hoping for this version, because I had never made any promises about watching that one.

"The Adrian Lyne. It's spectacular."

I breathed out. I was spending the night with Jeremy Irons and Melanie Griffith. "Sure, I'll microwave some popcorn."

—

We settled in front of the soft glow of his screen. The movie seemed only to be tinged with color, at moments it felt sepia. Melanie Griffith was equal parts trashy and vulnerable. Jeremy Irons was dashing and empathetic. And Dominique Swain, in the titular role, was . . . young. She looked really young. Her blond hair was in braids for most of the film, short shirts and rompers, saddle shoes. Red lipstick, often smeared.

"She was only fourteen when they started filming," he whispered to me, his breath salty and warm.

After it was over, Nick started to paw at my thigh. "I'm still sore from yesterday," I said, picking up the stray buttery kernels that had fallen onto his carpet. "Let's just go to sleep? I have to work in the morning."

The movie played through my head all night. Something

felt unsettled, but I couldn't figure out what or why. In the morning, Nick asked me if I liked it.

"It was really beautiful cinematography. Very arty."

"Great performances too, right?" He slurped his tea.

"Totally." I nodded into my cup. "Very empathic. And convincing."

"I don't get what people think the big deal is. Lolita was playing him the whole time."

The hot tea settled on my tongue. I didn't swallow.

Nick continued. "He loves her so much. When he begs her to go back with him, she's crazy to say no."

I swished around the lukewarm liquid and swallowed.

"Right. She's crazy. I mean, it makes no sense." The cup clinked as it hit the saucer. "I've got a long drive. See you later?" I kissed him on the cheek as I slung my backpack over my shoulder and left.

—

During the car ride to the day camp, I didn't play any music. The highway lay out in front of me, clogged with other cars filled with warm bodies, everyone with an intention and a purpose. I sat in traffic, checking my watch, trying to estimate the number of minutes I would be late. Why was I even staying at his place during the week? A half-hour drive home turned into an hour drive to work. I hated driving. And Nick would never drive me, even though he had nothing to do— another teacher from Hunt, Mr. Edwards, the one that had made him jealous, was the director of the program. When he found out I needed a summer job, he offered me a position.

I didn't even have to interview. If he spotted Nick across the parking lot even once, it would be disaster.

I thought about how Lolita left Humbert. How she chose to go with Quilty instead, to escape. It wasn't a great choice for a lot of reasons, but still, she left Humbert.

If Mr. Edwards knew, it would all be over with me and Nick. I wondered what Mr. Edwards would do if I told him, what he would say. I tried to imagine his face. Would he be surprised? Would he think I was lying? Did he know all along, like how other teachers seemed to know about each other? Did he not care?

Traffic began to relax. I pressed on the gas, softly. I pursed my lips and breathed out, wishing we had made coffee that morning instead of just boiling water for tea. My head hurt. I was still sore. I tried to adjust my hips against the sticky tan leather, but it didn't help. I was trapped in my car, in traffic, in the choices I had made. I would never find out what Mr. Edwards's reaction would be.

11

He got mad at me if I didn't come. Our new routine: Nick made gimlets and cosmos, he unwrapped me to my underwear, another cosmo, a sheer bra and matching thong was his favorite, another round of drinks, he didn't like lace, he'd rather have something silky to remove, dark towels at the ready, he was always on top. I still hurt. I didn't tell him to stop. But I bled only sometimes now.

He knew I was on the pill and had only been with other virgins before, always with condoms, because pregnancy terrified me. I had no idea how many other women he had been with. I asked once and he just laughed. I guessed that meant a lot.

I doubted if he discerned the meanings of my noises—this moan means *go*, that means *stop*, an inhale of *please*, my nails were *really, please stop*—I knew what to echo from that scene in *When Harry Met Sally* . . . when Meg Ryan pretends to have an orgasm and shocks Billy Crystal. Nick never questioned if "it was good for me too." At a certain point in the summer, as we got closer to the time when I would leave for Ithaca for what might as well be forever, I realized my pleasure was up to me. I read *Cosmopolitan* magazine, the sex column especially, with a certain focus. I needed to *tell my man what I want, or how can I expect an orgasm? Men aren't psychic!* the magazine's editors informed me. The next Friday over dinner I had an extra cosmo and as I downed the last of it, I smiled tightly and awkwardly started the conversation:

"I think you need to go down on me sometimes."

I immediately regretted that I finished my drink.

He almost choked on his chicken with laughter.

"You never let me."

Which was true. I had never let him kiss me lower than my hip tattoo, the star, I always pulled him northbound. I had a distinct disillusionment about my own body; I had never seen another girl fully nude, really, except once in a porn I watched with a bunch of girls on pay-per-view TV during an eighth-grade sleepover, and so I was unreasonably terrified there could be something wrong between my legs. I had no actual reason to believe this; I had been to the gynecologist and had my bikini waxed by a professional multiple times at that point. The comments by each were only as such:

"Your uterus is tipped! No big deal."

"My, not much to remove. Let's see what we can do, though."

"You're a perfectly healthy pink. Do you need a refill on your script?"

There was no reason for these fears, but nonetheless, I

was certain something could be wrong with me. Why else did I still bleed sometimes during sex? Why else did it hurt so much? Wasn't this supposed to be fun the whole time? It never occurred to me even for a second that maybe the sex I was having with the teacher was too rough, too unkind, that I was unprepared in every way and so had the opposite of a good time—pain and blood. This thought never even began to flower.

So that night I got exceptionally drunk, and when he pushed me onto the floor and his kisses turned southbound I squeezed my eyes shut and braced myself, convinced he would be revolted by me. I was nauseated, from stress and vodka. I pressed my eyelids with my hands and waited for something to happen. His mouth was warm and his hands were on my hips but nothing was happening inside me. *Isn't something supposed to happen?* I thought, reaching in my mind for the rest of that article I read—shouldn't I just start having an orgasm now? Our sex had never been so quiet. It sounded awful. My mouth began to fill with saliva and I began to feel something, but it was the certain possibility that I might throw up.

"Oh my God, stop!" I sat up and gagged, I held the carpet and the room still moved.

"What the fuck, Alisson?" He was too loud, I realized that immediately. Even in my dizzy state I realized he was far too loud for this late at night with the windows open. Sometimes before bed we could hear the murmur of the downstairs neighbor's television. Those same neighbors could certainly hear Nick yelling now.

"I just—I'm not—" I tried to hold still. I breathed the saliva back in, I willed my stomach to stay inside. He yelled again, loud enough now that the neighbors could surely hear—

"I was licking your asshole!"

There was nowhere deep enough inside myself to crawl to get away from those words.

Not only was that absolutely *not* enjoyable but it wasn't even what I wanted. *Is that what oral sex is?* I thought. *Is that always what oral sex has to be? Should I have loved that?* What was wrong with me? Everything began to race inside. And now, now, it was happening—the swelling, pressure on my sternum, I choked on my own breathing, I couldn't keep it together at all. What I would now understand as a panic attack. At the time I thought I was going to die. The room was dark, there were candles, and I could see him standing over me, yanking up the blankets and his clothes and stomping back and forth to his bedroom until I was alone, bottomless with only a bra, on his carpet.

He knocked over the last of my drink in the martini glass, swore at me about the carpet, and threw the glass against the wall. A hundred shards exploded into light in the dark. I pressed my mouth closed hard with my hands and hoped that if I was still enough, I would become invisible.

He was still partially dressed and I heard the front door slam behind him. But I couldn't see the glass in the dark, I was barefoot and bare bodied. So I just hiccuped and watched the moon.

At some point he came back inside. I was exactly as he'd left me. He now had canvas flip-flops on.

"I want to go home," I said.

He came to me, scooped me up, and I started crying quietly, and he carried me to the bedroom. He pushed my hair out of my face and pressed his mouth into my neck, next to my ear, and poured out, all at once, "I love you so much, I'm so in love with you, I would never hurt you," and it began to merge and muddle, so I knew he meant it. And we made up very gently. And in the early morning light I found all the shards of glass and collected them in a paper bag, and I knew where the vacuum was already. I used a sponge for the sticky pink on the wall from the last of the drink, foamed the stain on the carpet, and let it soak. By 8:00 A.M. everything was exactly as it was before I had that stupid idea.

When he came out of the bedroom, he had a six-page letter for me. He boiled water and left me in the living room to read it. It started: *I don't think you understand my reaction last night so I will attempt to explain. I may be a little vivid and crass but there's no other way to explain myself. . . . When you stop me, it makes me feel like I am bad at it or that you don't like it or that I am hurting you or that you're uncomfortable with me or a combination of some or all of those things . . . it frustrates me because you are punishing yourself on purpose . . . and it's bullshit because you end up punishing me. You take my enjoyment out of it and (forgive me for saying it) all my hard work is for nothing. . . . Last night, I knew that you were a little sore and so I was being really gentle . . . and then you got all mean and angry and that* *was that. . . . I hadn't done anything wrong and so, while I <u>was</u> being a puppy dog, I didn't apologize because I was only trying to make you happy and in turn make me happy and you took that power and threw it in my face. . . . I'm still not happy because we ruined a very nice night. We still need to talk about openness to sex things and we need to do it soon so that such a possibly fun thing doesn't turn out to ruin you and me. . . . Your lover, Nick*

I left for college the following week.

12

It wasn't always like that. There were times we stayed up all night counting the stars we'd draw on paper and then in the sky, making up our own constellations. Or he'd play a song, sitting on the floor with his guitar on his lap, trying out lyrics, saying how this one was gonna be about me. He showed me how to make his grandmother's chicken soup, the secret was a pinch of curry to give it color, and he fed it to me spoonful by spoonful. He'd say I was beautiful more than anyone ever had before. How I was worth the wait. Over and over. There were nights we spent with his voice as the only sound, him reading to me his favorite Dickens novels. His fingers trailing the waves in my Alice-in-Wonderland hair, calling me Dinah between slow kisses. Or fantasizing together how our future would unfold—the next year, him at Cornell, us together. Two college students in love. Then he could kiss me whenever, wherever I wanted, on the street, in a coffee shop, at the movies. Those times were so sweet and sincere, they felt true. Those times were why I loved him. And why I never questioned when he said he loved me.

13

The first thing I did when I got to college was fuck a stranger. Orientation Weekend, classes on Monday, anticipation crawling across the quad. Over the summer, whenever I had stayed late at the day camp with other counselors, waiting for some child's busy parents or a forgetful babysitter, all the younger counselors like me, no longer high school seniors but not yet college freshmen, would listen to the older counselors wax on about college.

"You can do whatever you want, man," this older boy, Shane, told me as he double-checked his attendance roster for the day, making sure he hadn't miscounted. "No parents, no rules."

"Aren't there, like, hall counselors or whatever?" I countered.

"RAs," he corrected. "They're your friend. Or not. Whatever. They're still not your mom. They're just juniors or seniors and narc on you if they catch you with beer or smoking. Some don't care, though."

"Aren't there professors? Like, they must care," I said, putting crayons back in their yellow cardboard homes.

Shane shrugged. "There are some classes where the prof doesn't even know my name, the class is so big. Lectures."

I shook the crayon box, creating room for one more.

"You know what the best part is, though?"

"What?" I asked, hopeful.

"The sex."

I soured my face at him, suddenly aware he might be hitting on me. He was cute, but not that cute.

"For real, I just mean like, there's no sneaking around. There's no like . . ." He looked for a word. "Judgment. There's no judgment. It's not like when you're a kid and you have sex with someone and you're going to get married. You can have sex with whoever you want and it's no big deal. They give away condoms like candy."

"Huh." I stacked crayon boxes into their basket.

"Being single in college is the only way to go," he concluded. "Those guys who try to make it work with some girl long distance—it's a joke. It never works out. And they just get all mopey and skip class and it's because they realized what they're missing out on."

I pulled my hands through my hair and redid my ponytail. "Good thing I'm single then, huh?"

"Yeah, Ali. You're single." His voice winked at me.

I cleared my throat. "Excuse me?"

"It's so obvious you've got a boyfriend, or something. You,

like, ignore the guys here." He must have seen my face turn. "Don't worry, it's not like people care *that* much."

He leaned over the picnic table, the wood grayed and smooth from sun and rain. "I can keep a secret, though, if you want."

I tightened my gaze at him. "I don't have a boyfriend."

He laughed, raising his hands and shaking them. "Okay, Ali. Okay. For real, though"—suddenly serious, a little sad, as if he understood this deeply—"it's not gonna work out. You'll regret that you wasted your time."

—

Weeks later, I was on a campus full of strangers. The girls living in my hall were all loud and caked on their eyeliner, and although everyone was a freshman, somehow there was always beer. Cheap beer, sometimes lukewarm beer, but beer. Beer when you put on your makeup, beer when you took the elevator down eleven floors, beer wherever you arrived as soon as you walked in.

I met a boy the first night at a blowout party I went to with my hallmates, my geographic girlfriends. I had never been at a party like that before. Loud music, kegs, so much yelling. It seemed like any party I went to in high school was always trying to restrain itself, keep it together, plausible deniability. At college, it was go big or go home. His name was Ted. He told me he was a wrestler, and he had acne scars on his face. He was blond. "Oh, he's so *cute!*" my new hallmates/ girlfriends encouraged me as they similarly paired off. "Totally go for it!"

—

Only a few days before I left home, the last night I stayed with Nick, he had told me again, "I don't want you to miss anything."

It was dark, I was trying to stay up all night, but I just wanted to sleep. Packing was impossible. How could I fit my entire life into a dorm room? Into only enough boxes to fit in my mom's station wagon?

"I know," I whispered back, squeezing his arm. I shoved my face into the pillow. "I know."

He shook me. "Ali, this is important. College is so important, you deserve it more than anyone. You earned it." He was sitting up now. "I don't want to keep you from any of it."

I ran my hand against his face, the dull stubble. "I love you," I said.

"I love you too. Are you sure this is what you want?"

"Oh my God, yes, *yes*, how many times do we have to talk about this?" I picked up the pillow and pushed it on top of my face now and screamed into it, "I need to *sleep*."

"Okay, okay, okay. Go to sleep then."

"Thank you." I rolled away from him, the trails of sunrise on the wall.

"I just don't want you to miss anything," his voice said again, the last thing I heard.

—

Ted asked me what kind of beer I wanted. "Whatever!" I yelled into his ear over the music. I wasn't sure what I wanted to do, but I was sure I wanted a beer. Like everyone else. I wanted to be like everyone else and this was my chance. I didn't want it to be like high school. I didn't want to miss things anymore.

Three red plastic cups of beer later, I kissed Ted, and when he took my hand, I followed him out of the party, across the quad, into his empty room. Ted slurred his words, there were no I love yous, only a "Wow" as he cupped my right breast, a soft "You're so pretty" as he kissed my neck.

The sex was fast but gentle. I didn't have to brace myself. Instead of holding me too tight, his hands were soft. It was like all my high school boyfriends. I missed that. I watched the slow-moving stars through the window. I was definitely drunk. I squeezed my eyes shut when he came and then he immediately followed it by saying he was sorry.

I thought of Nick in that last moment, Ted's arms around me, his leg tucked in between mine, all in an effort to make us fit together on a twin bed. I realized I wasn't in pain. The awareness of the absence made my eyes focus for a second, the stars on the other side of the window sharpen.

I woke up to the sunrise, shoved against the cold heating grate on the concrete wall. Ted was passed out on his stomach next to me. I had to vomit. I grabbed his T-shirt on the floor to wear to the boys' bathroom, barefoot. After, I crawled back into my own clothes and found my lanyard with my room key next to, thank God, a condom wrapper. I thought about kissing Ted goodbye for a second but then felt another wave of nausea.

I didn't understand what I had done, only that I knew I could never tell Nick.

—

Later that morning, the other girls in my hall, who were fast becoming best friends with each other, were *so* excited for me going home with Ted. "Oh my Gawd, he was so cute!" they exclaimed over dining hall pancakes, some still in the clothes from the night before, joining us straight from another stranger's dorm room. They didn't know about Nick.

I sketched stars on my plate with maple syrup. "Yeah," I agreed. "He's really sweet, too." The girls cooed.

"But I don't think it's going to work out," I said as I picked out the best forkful of pancake. "Like, he's just not my type."

A wave of nods went around the table. "Plus," one girl added, "it's just the first weekend! There's so many cute guys here—you don't want to stick with the first one you meet. Maybe you'll meet someone in a class."

I nodded back. "Totally."

From then on, Ted and I would wave and talk briefly whenever we ran into each other: *How's the team? Oh, great. What a crazy snowstorm last night! Right?* But that was it. I didn't understand what was supposed to be so great about hooking up.

I found myself hearing Nick's voice over and over those first days, weeks. Did him not wanting me to miss anything mean he wanted me to cheat on him? Yeah, right. He had already been calling every day, asking me lots of questions about who I was spending my time with, where I was, *oh, tell me more about him* if I mentioned a name that sounded like a boy.

If he actually meant it, though, that would mean breaking up. I didn't want to date anyone here or even hook up with anyone else. The fact that this had happened, that I had *cheated on my boyfriend*, coiled inside me like a hot metal chain. I knew if I told him, Nick would be mad. I knew he'd yell. Maybe he would even break up with me. If I told him in person, I didn't know what he would do. So I never told him. I never started that conversation, about what I had done to him or to ask what he really meant. *I don't want you to miss anything.* But what I missed most was him.

14

My first semester at Ithaca College was empty, socially, on purpose—other than that first hookup, I didn't engage in any way with boys. Or even girls, really. The fact that I was dating a teacher from my high school wasn't the kind of secret I could share, the kind of gossip I could trade. Nick had made it clear, over and over, how *screwed* he would be if anyone found out, how he would not only get fired but never be able to get another job teaching again, how *no one could understand us.* And there were a handful of students from my high school here at college with me, including my theater friend Richie, so it was imperative that no one at college found out either. Even though I was now a five-hour drive away.

I still had disability status because of my insomnia, so I got a single dorm room. There was no need to explain to anyone why I was waiting by the phone late at night. I couldn't call Nick, though. My parents paid the phone bill and so could see what numbers I dialed. But they didn't see who called me. So I would wait.

Every week, Thursday, Friday, and Saturday nights, the girls in my hall would all get ready together to go out to parties. All dozen of us, always. I'd join in for the dress-up part; I'd hold my door open with a textbook and let the dialogue from an episode of *Sex and the City*, on in another girl's room, leak into my room as I prowled through my closet.

"This one?" I asked Kelly, the Long Island brunette, about a tiny Abercrombie & Fitch T-shirt with some saying about "chicks" on it that Nick bought for me.

"No," she told me, and walked into my room and assessed my closet with the supreme confidence of knowing what college boys liked. She pulled out a tinier tank top, no matter how cold it was that night. "This."

I'd stand with the pack of girls in the bathroom, all of our makeup spread out above the sinks, eye shadow shimmer in blues and browns dusting the white porcelain. I was good at putting on makeup from years of theater, but the girls in my hall were better. Except for one girl, Heather. Heather barely wore ChapStick. So I began helping her with her eyeliner. "Look up!" I'd direct, using three shades of eye shadow to bring out her eyes. They were big and brown, and she had nice skin if she put on a little powder to mask the oil on her nose. She always thanked me and promised to get me a drink later that night to pay me back.

Another girl, Tiffany, would take photos of us, coaxing us into a group in the middle of our hallway, right by the elevator.

I learned she didn't have a uterus when I knocked on her door once for a spare tampon.

"Oh, I don't get a period!" as she explained. Instead of a simple *no*. I wasn't used to that level of honesty and acceptance. Just, *This is my body! And it's totally okay!* It was the opposite of my experience. Once, months later, we were talking about being future moms, and she told me that she had just always known, years before doctors noticed she didn't have a uterus, that she was meant to adopt children. I was envious of someone who could be so certain about something so important.

Nick had said it would be at least another year until we could tell any of our families or friends back home, even after he came back to Cornell. How much longer than that would I have to wait for what followed? How could we get married and have kids if we couldn't even hold each other's hands in public yet? I was already tired of lying.

The girls and I would spend hours, literally hours, in our shared bathroom and hallway changing clothes and doing our hair, giving opinions and talking about what party we were going to and what boy would be there, taking photos with disposable cameras right until we called a taxi. The good parties were always off campus.

And then, after the taxi was called, maybe just as it arrived, I would have a headache, or had a paper I forgot about but *really* had to start working on, or was suddenly *so tired*. And the girls would hug me and leave for the party, promising to tell me all about it the next day, and I would move my math-book doorstop and let my door swing shut. And, with all my makeup on, hair dried and pinned, in a push-up bra and short skirt, I'd wait for Nick to call me, fingering the twisted plastic coils of the phone from my bed.

I still wasn't writing, and no one would have cared anyway. The school was so much bigger than Hunt, a whole campus, with quads to cross. But it was familiar too: no one noticed where I was. No one was waiting for me. No one saw me, it seemed. Even my hallmates didn't care why I ended up not coming along. *One less body to fit in a car,* I was sure they thought. Was that what I missed most? The attention? That idea made me feel sick.

I imagined that maybe Nick was just as lonely in school as I was. Maybe he missed me too. *I don't want you to miss out on anything.* At first when he said it I thought it was sweet, gentle, even generous. Now it felt like it was following me around, a snake hissing at my feet. It began to feel like a warning.

I'm just being paranoid, I thought, feeling guilty about Ted. About the moments when I wasn't missing Nick. *I shouldn't go out, I'm more than just a stupid college girl who wants to get drunk,* I told myself, *I have a boyfriend who loves me and is waiting for me. I should be more grateful. I'm not missing anything. If Nick really wanted me to experience college life like normal, we wouldn't have stayed together. He knows better than me, and I need to trust him.*

That was how I convinced myself, day after day, that his words were about love, not control.

15

It wasn't until the first long weekend of the semester, Columbus Day, that Nick drove up to Ithaca after school on Friday. I hadn't seen him in a month. Over the summer, we had made so many plans—the things we would do each weekend, the acoustic band that would be playing one night, the art show opening, where we would go to eat. Over the summer, I collected colored pamphlets from places we went, listing future activities in my head, delighting over the options. But once the semester started, plans fell through week after week. Nick had more grading than he thought, then his parents were in town, then he was just exhausted, and so on. Freshmen weren't allowed to have cars, so our plans were built onto his.

Still taking care not to be seen, we wouldn't embrace until my dorm room door shut behind us.

"I have missed you *so* much, Ali," he said into my hair.

"So, so much." His hands immediately went to the button of my jeans.

"Hey—" I took hold of his hands. "I've missed you too." I closed my mouth and looked at him, a moment of quiet. His face looked the same. "Can't we just talk first?"

"Ali, we talk all the time."

"Yeah, but it's always so late and you've got to get to school in the morning, so . . . I don't know." My arms tightened into each other behind my back. "I just want to, like, reconnect?"

"Uh, what better way to reconnect than . . ." He reached for my jeans again, laughing. I smacked his hand away from my button. I took a sharp inhale and began speaking before I could think it through.

"For real. Half the time you don't call me when you say you will, and when you do you're usually grumpy and just want me to listen to you jerk off. That's not a relationship." I heard my own voice but didn't recognize it. I watched his face turn and his eyes tighten.

"You've got to be kidding me. I just drove over five hours to see you." He threw up his hands and let his backpack drop to the floor. "God, you're so immature sometimes."

I felt my ribs knit into each other. I started crying, the wordless, fixing-onto-something-invisible-in-front-of-you kind. He kept yelling sentences I didn't process, then stormed out, leaving his backpack. I sat on my twin bed in the silence that remained. I had hoped maybe he would bring flowers, that we could sit on my bed and talk for hours, he would tell me about school and I could tell him how much I hated Italian and missed my cats.

It was already so cold out you could see your breath at night. It hadn't snowed, but everyone knew it was coming. In my slippers, I took the long elevator ride down, found him leaning on his parked car smoking a cigarette. The image was familiar, even if it was in a different state. I walked into his body, his arms wrapping around me out of habit.

"I forgot my coat," I mumbled into his.

"Yeah," he said, exhaling. "I know."

—

We slept in my twin bed that night. We didn't fit well. It hadn't seemed to bother Ted, though, who had at least tried to make room. Nick was too big, even though I was so small I tucked myself under his arm. He complained about how he never had to deal with these kinds of things, since he was in a frat and all and had full-size beds.

"Yeah," I reminded him. "I know."

—

The next morning we got bagels in town and drove home to his apartment. I had lied to my parents, something nonspecific about too much homework, needing to study, so I was staying put on campus. Everything awkward about the night before was forgotten. We were driving and it felt fun and easy again like the summer. We sang along to the radio, stopped at the Roscoe Diner for lunch, he held my hand as he drove. I remembered how lucky I was. My boyfriend was hot and smart and had a whole life—a job, a car, an apartment, a cat. And he adored me. He didn't stop telling me he loved me the whole day.

I brought his favorite lingerie that he said I looked really sexy in. The raspberry lip gloss that was his favorite. I shaved my legs again that morning in the dorm communal bathroom before we left. I did all the things I knew he'd like.

We got home, to his home, and he ordered us a pizza and started making drinks. A cosmo, he had bought another bottle of the pink mix just for me.

"Pink for my Lolita," he said as he handed me the glass. Ever since the martini glass broke, he gave me my drink in a regular glass, no rocks. The change was never mentioned.

We clinked *to us*. We finished our drinks. He made another round. The pizza arrived. I kept drinking. He made another round. I kept drinking. He pulled off my dress. He liked the lingerie I chose. It felt like we were dancing in his living room, but there wasn't music. I fell to my knees, this was more drinking than usual for me, and since I had gone to college my stomach wasn't used to more than beer. I wanted to throw up. He told me he wanted a blow job. I told him not now, I was going to be sick. We weren't dancing anymore, but the room was still moving. He picked me up like a child, carried me into his bedroom, gently putting me onto the bed.

He took a pillow and put it on the floor next to the bed frame. "Can't hold your liquor, my darling?" He picked me up again and set me on the floor, leaning me onto the frame, knees on the pillow. "You've got to learn to drink like a lady."

There was a mirror over the closet door, in front of me, right next to the bed. If I leaned over, I could touch the glass with the tips of my fingers. Leaning was dangerous at that moment, though. I saw myself still in my reflection. It looked like everything was moving but me. The overhead light was off, but the bedside lamps were on. The room glowed and morphed in and out of darkness. I saw him take off his pants. He talked the whole time, telling me step by step what he was doing, telling me to remember this for next time, that it was time he taught me. That I needed to learn. It wasn't something I had done with him. I tried talking, but words weren't working. He knelt down for a moment, kissed me hard, opened my mouth with his tongue and hooked between my teeth with his thumb, and then shoved his dick inside, his hand on my head like I was a puppet and he was the strings. He turned and stared at himself in the full-length mirror, making grunts and moans, and I kept saying over and over to myself, *Don't throw up, don't throw up, don't throw up,* with my eyes closed. He put his hand around my throat and cheek, moved his hips so that if I opened my eyes, I could stare at my empty body in the mirror, my mouth filled with his dick. He talked about how much he liked watching me do this to him.

It seemed to go on forever. Watching this happen to me felt like I was someone else, this wasn't my body, this wasn't him, this wasn't my fantasy of us at all. This had never happened before. At once, the urge to vomit overcame me and I fell forward, away. Nick grunted and grabbed his dick— "What the fuck, Ali"—and I reached out to catch myself, my hand pressed onto the cold silver pane of the looking glass, and I saw what was happening to me in the mirror. I threw up onto his floor. In the rabbit hole of the relationship, I couldn't understand how I got here or what was wrong with this love story. But I remembered everything like he asked.

16

There must have been a moment when Pandora opened the box and realized what she had done. It was already too late—everything awful in the world pouring out in front of her—but there must have been a moment after it began when she understood the error of judgment. That the exchange—this for that, curiosity for reality—was not fair. This wasn't what she wanted. I wonder how she felt, as it all happened in front of her: Was it panic? Fear? Shame? Did she desperately wish she had made a different choice? Did she wish someone were there to rescue her? Or did she realize she was all alone now, and it was her fault?

We have no idea what Lolita thought in the moment when she decided to leave Humbert. Nabokov wrote from the perspective of Humbert in his diaries, already on trial for murder. Everything we know about Dolores Haze is colored by his gaze; even her name, Lolita, is his creation. Humbert rarely calls her Dolores. Even so—she leaves him. She escapes.

To him, it is a mystery, clearly she was kidnapped by another man, she was taken advantage of, she was coerced. He cannot imagine that she left him of her own accord. But that's not what happened in the reality of the story. There must have been some moment when she realized, *I don't want to be with him anymore*, and then she took the steps needed to go. She fled, she got out. Let's not focus yet on where she ended up.

I wish I could write down that this was my moment, the night when I saw myself in the mirror. The night when he told me I needed to remember all of it. I wish I could tell you that that was my final straw, the line was crossed, I understood things would only get worse, that I recognized the signs of an abusive relationship, and that I cut off contact from him, never saw him again, found my happy ending in Ithaca after all. But that's not this story.

Reader, I stayed.

17

I spent most of the semester overwhelmed. I wanted more than anything to prove myself wrong, to prove everyone wrong in high school who thought I would never succeed, much less graduate. I wrote the papers, read whole books in a weekend, and struggled to learn Italian. I didn't like the class, but Nick had convinced me to take it. He was Italian and he said it would be romantic if we could go to Italy some-day, maybe on a honeymoon. He didn't really speak Italian, though. It wasn't as much like Latin as I hoped it would be.

I began to darken. I never knew when I would hear from Nick and spent most nights in my room, waiting. I had a small TV with a DVD player, but no cable. I watched Baz Luhrmann's *Romeo + Juliet* over and over. I had isolated my-self on purpose, I hadn't made many friends, other than my hallmates, kind of. They could hear when Nick and I got into fights on the phone, they saw him come in and out of my room the occasional weekend he visited, but I never answered any questions about him and wouldn't gossip over late-night tacos like everyone else. I'd shrug, *he's just a guy from my high school*, vague responses that weren't memorable. I hated lying. It was easier not to talk.

As the semester lurched forward, visits happened less and less often. I was entirely dependent on his schedule, his time, his car. There was one weekend that caused a huge fight, when he decided at the last minute to go to his friend's party instead of visiting. He said he couldn't just make up an excuse and lie to his friend like that, so he had to go. We screamed at each other over the phone and didn't talk again for two days.

The following week I didn't get my period.

I didn't tell him immediately. I didn't want him to think I was a dramatic teenager. I spent those days trying to keep as focused on my work as possible but finding myself writing my future married name in the margins of my notebook: *Mrs. Alisson Marie North*. Or just staring out windows, watching the wind rattle through the trees.

I knew we'd end up getting married anyway, getting pregnant would just make things happen faster. I had always assumed we would have children eventually. Nick was Catholic, abortion wasn't even an option. I imagined myself in a white dress, belly blooming with child, being married in front of our friends and family, people cooing over how cute I was in my veil, congratulating Nick on our future happiness. *People will have to know. You can only hide a pregnancy for so long.*

I could finish college later. Or maybe I wouldn't. But I wasn't interested in that version of my future, of being a

stay-at-home mom, of never getting a degree. I would probably not become a writer, then, much less an actress. All I
would get was Nick. Maybe he would want me to get an
abortion after all. I had heard a friend of my mother's once say
that when it comes to abortion, guys say one thing and then
another when it's their problem. I made a big box around my
possible future name and filled it in with blue ink. At eighteen, I didn't know what I wanted.

I hoped he wouldn't get upset. I was on the pill, but
when I'd drink too much, I'd throw up or go to sleep without taking it. It wasn't consistent enough to offer me the full
potential protection. I wasn't dumb; I knew pregnancy was
possible. But when I brought condoms up, he asked me if I
was cheating on him.

"No, *never*," I assured him.

I finally told him on the phone after leaving him an IM
in the morning: *we need to talk. it's an emergency.* He called
me as soon as school was out, on the pay phone in the parking lot. I blurted it out without any nuance—"I think I'm
pregnant." He got really quiet. I cried yet again.

But then he came alive with caring. "Ali, it's okay, it's going
to be okay, don't cry, we'll get through this together." He told
me he would come visit this weekend, rearrange everything to
see me. He told me he loved me and we would be okay.

"Okay," I told him. He listened to me cry, waited for me
to calm down.

"So the soonest I can be there is Friday night. Is that okay
for you? I'll get us a hotel. It's okay if you have to study this
time, it's important."

"Okay, yeah."

"I love you," he reminded me. "I love you."

"I love you too, Nick." He called me again that night. We talked until late, not about the fears but about how much he missed me.

I went to sleep the easiest I had in weeks, knowing everything he was doing to take care of me. I felt like I could get through this, no matter what.

The next morning I woke up with blood on my sheets. I got my period after all. There was no emergency. It felt like a knot in my body untied all at once, the anxiety of having to make a choice I had no interest in making expelled from my body.

I didn't tell him when he called me again that afternoon after school. Or the next day. Or the next. Every time we spoke, I wanted to, I knew I should, but a ball fixed itself in my throat and all I could do was listen to his voice tell me how much he cared about me. I wanted to see him so badly. He was acting in ways he hadn't in weeks, months, since I left. He suddenly remembered what classes I was taking, the name of the girl down the hall who vaguely resembled a cheerleader from Hunt. I didn't want his attention to fade away. I drew hearts and rewrote my future name over and over again as we talked: *Mrs. Alisson Marie North.* I imagined a bouquet, a minister, white rice, our friends and family cheering when we kissed. Part of me wished I hadn't gotten my period at all. I gnawed on my mouth when I listened to him say "I love you."

I knew it couldn't last, though. When he came to visit,

he'd want to have sex, and he'd notice the blood. I IM'ed him Friday morning, *just got it*, knowing he would stop at home before he started driving, that he would see it. He called me when he got home.

"I'm so relieved!"

"I know, me too," I said.

"Now we can relax. Thank God," he said. "The last thing I wanted to do was drive ten hours this weekend."

"Wait—you're not coming?"

"Ali, I was making the stretch for you because of, you know . . . but I really don't have that kind of time right now. You know grades are due next week and—"

"Right, of course. Hey, I have to go and meet some friends to study."

"Love you, Ali. I'm really glad we're okay."

"Me too," I said.

After we hung up, I lay down on my bed, turned on a heating pad, and pulled the blanket over me. I put on *Romeo + Juliet*. I didn't talk to anyone the rest of the night. When the girls knocked on my door for dinner, I didn't answer.

18

Nick knew I wasn't happy. He wasn't stupid. When we would get to see each other, we'd have sex, but I stopped pretending to like it. It became horribly quiet.

"Are you asleep?"

I scrunched my face against the pillow. "No."

He slowed down. "What's wrong?"

What was wrong was that it physically hurt and I was tired of hurting. I liked the closeness, how he'd tell me he loved me and kiss me. But the actual act of sex? It was over-ripe with pain.

"Nothing, I love you. Don't stop."

He didn't.

—

After, he ran his finger on my arm. "Hey."

I knew he wanted to talk about it. The effort of

performance—during sex, for this conversation, even over dinner—was too much.

"Hey yourself."

"Don't you love me?"

"What?" I sat up. "Yes, what are you—"

"Well, if you don't want me to fuck you anymore—"

"That is *not* what I said—I didn't say anything."

He got out of bed. "Well, what's wrong with you, then?"

My deepest, darkest fear. There was something wrong with me. That's why it hurt, that's why I didn't ever have an orgasm, that's why I couldn't enjoy it like I was supposed to. He wasn't a virgin like my other boyfriends, he knew what he was doing. I was the one with the problem. But I wanted him to think he was a problem too.

"Well, maybe you're not as great as you think you are," I said instead.

"Excuse me?"

"It's because you're fat." I blurted it out and knew before I finished the word how awful I was. He was standing in front of the window, his body outlined by the moon. He sucked in his stomach.

"You're fucking kidding me, Ali."

He wasn't really fat. He wasn't really in shape either. He had a slight paunch in his midsection, and I had never seen him exercise. But his body was the same, nothing had changed.

"Maybe you're not as hot as you think you are." My mouth was just moving at this point and I knew what I was saying was unforgivable. I was willing to say anything. Anything that wasn't about how I knew something awful was wrong with me, how I was the broken one.

He sat next to me on the bed, his stomach rolling over his boxers. "I'm sorry I can't look like you want me to," he said, his shoulders down, wounded.

I didn't expect that reaction. I rubbed his back. "It's okay, it's stupid. I love you. I'm being shallow."

"Can we just go to sleep?"

"Yeah, sure." And I curled up next to him, my hand going to his stomach, his soft fur, like every night we were together. He pushed my hand away.

19

I finished the semester with almost straight A's, a lone B plus in Italian that I worked hard for. I was home for more than a month for break. I wore the ring Nick had given me over the summer, the tiny diamond glinting whenever I moved my hand. Nick told me I shouldn't wear it, but I didn't care. I desperately wanted to tell someone. I wanted Nick to tell someone. I wanted people to know.

"It's not a big deal anymore. I graduated. I'm eighteen. Why are you constantly freaking out about this?" I almost-yelled at him one night over break.

"You don't get it, Ali, you never did. You have no idea what I risk every damn day to love you," he said as he finished his second Humbert cocktail that night.

I was so tired of him telling me what I did and did not know.

"Whatever. I'm going to bed," I said, leaving my drink on the table. "I'm really tired."

He fixed himself another drink. I washed my face in cold water, knowing I needed to calm down. I *was* tired. I was tired from school. I was tired of lying. I was tired of our fights. I felt trapped in my own mouth, in his apartment, in the secrets.

I went back into the living room. "Well, anyway, I think my sister knows."

I heard the knife slam against the cutting board. More limes. "What?" His voice ice cold.

"I think Lauren knows."

He came into the living room as I sat down on the couch, twirling the ring on my hand. "I didn't tell her anything, she just noticed the ring and was like, 'Oh, where'd you get that, Ali?' and I was like, 'Nowhere,' and she was like, 'Oh, so who gave it to you?' and I was like, 'None of your beeswax,' and she was all, 'Uh-huh, sure, I bet it was a guy,' and I told her it wasn't and she didn't believe me and then just started naming my ex-boyfriends and I was like, 'No way, stop,' and then she named you and I just . . ."

"You what?" He was still standing in the doorway.

"I told her it was not Mr. North and she needed to keep her dumb ideas to herself. She must have heard those rumors last year." I picked up my abandoned drink. "It's fine."

He started yelling, how could I do this to him, how could I be so stupid, so careless. I yelled back, how could he do this to *me*, I was so sick of hiding, and it was obviously because he didn't actually love me at all. At some point another drink appeared.

"You know what, Ali, if you can't take this seriously, then I won't take you seriously. How about that?"

"Fine. You don't even care about me at all, you just want to fuck a student." I realized I had gone too far before the words finished leaving my mouth, but the sentence finished itself.

He went silent. He threw back the rest of his drink and pulled on a coat and slammed the front door behind him, walking away from my apologies. It was snowing out. At first I thought he was just having a cigarette, he had done that before to cool off, but then I heard his car start.

I cleaned up the kitchen. Pulled on a T-shirt of his and boxers. I went to bed, petted his cat that was claiming his side of the bed for herself. Still, he didn't come back.

Eventually I fell asleep. I woke up suddenly, realizing he was standing over me, silent.

"Fuck, Nick."

He just looked at me.

"What?"

He spoke, quiet and soft. "You don't actually believe that? Right?"

"No, no, of course not. I was just mad. I'm sorry. I would never think that. Come to bed."

I held his head against my chest. His hands were still cold. He smelled like smoke. I fell asleep like that, and when I woke up, I was alone.

20

We wanted Christmas to be ours. Even with all the fighting, with how often my body began stiffening at his touch or his word, I found myself reaching out through the cold toward our fantasy of the holiday we could have together. I held fast.

It was a fantasy we had had for a year. When we were meeting only in diners and classrooms, he waxed on about how he would read *A Christmas Carol* aloud for his family, for his girlfriend, how much they loved it. I didn't really like Charles Dickens, but it seemed so pure and specific. As winter came, he would mention it and how he couldn't wait to share that with me. How we would have our own Christmas tree, hot chocolate while it snowed outside, gifts tied with bakery string by the fireplace, stockings hung with care.

I held fast to this hope, that maybe this could be the magic to make everything okay.

—

A week before Christmas, Nick drove us to a tree farm, not the one nearby since that's where everyone from town went, but one farther away. The hour drive didn't feel long at all, with classic Christmas carols on the radio and the snows-capes on the side of the road. It was beautiful.

"We'll cut our own," Nick said to the well-layered atten-dant, who handed him a slim saw. And off we went.

We trudged in the packed snow, our boots caught for a second with every step. Nick wore a tan A&F knit hat, and as time went on and my nose got colder, I suggested we look only a little longer before going back to the tree we liked a half hour ago. I said it sweetly, sotto voce, decidedly a ques-tion. I didn't want to push him. And he agreed, swinging the saw around his arm as we walked back and placed his cap on the tree. I had brought a disposable camera and snapped a photo. Another of Nick next to the tree. Then he took one of me across the snow.

"You know, let's just stick with this one," he said. He knelt down and pushed away the lowest branches, trying to find the best place to start sawing.

I squatted onto my heels, holding the green, sticky limbs off his body, and watched him force the saw through the trunk. He took breaks and kissed me on the nose.

Finally man overcame nature. I took a shot of him in tri-umph, and we laughed and I held up the treetop so it didn't drag as he carried the tree back to the entrance.

—

The night before Christmas Eve, I drove to his apartment for our own Christmas. I knew sneaking away from home on the actual holiday would be impossible, and he couldn't either, so we made the best of what we had.

"This makes it just for us," he said. I nodded back as I sipped cinnamon tea from his mug.

He read *A Christmas Carol*, doing voices just like he used to when he read to me at the diner. I had Duchess sleeping on my lap and the soft, velvety-sharp smell of the fresh-cut tree and didn't know how I could possibly be happier. In the morning, he gave me an early edition of *The Bell Jar* and a tiny music box that plinked out "Twinkle, Twinkle, Little Star." I unwrapped a set of martini glasses, a gift for me to live at his apartment. "The others weren't a set anyway, so this is even better," I said as I hugged him. I didn't comment that he was replacing his own glass, the one that he broke.

I had made him a soft pillow from flannel fabric, bought with an employee discount even though I didn't work at the fabric and crafts store anymore. I had made a pillow like that for every one of my high school boyfriends. My mother had to help me sew the corners. She didn't ask who it was for, just commented on the starry fabric.

We spent the day inside. He took a photo of me later, in the baby-blue lingerie set, a cosmo in my new martini glass. He kept the camera.

It wasn't until months later, looking through the photos that he kept in the chest of drawers in his bedroom, that I noticed—there were still no photographs of us. The same snowy backdrop, the same Christmas tree behind bodies. A sequence on film that couldn't be contrived. There's no way to look at it and not see what was going on. But still—no proof. The rule not broken.

21

I spent New Year's Eve with him. He made us a fancy dinner of roast chicken and mashed potatoes and green beans. We got champagne and had Dick Clark on TV. We talked about how the semester had gone for me.

"I'm so proud of you, Ali." He rubbed my hand. "You kicked ass."

"Yeah, I did, didn't I?" I smiled at him. "I really love my professors."

"Oh, really?" I caught a twinge in his voice, but the meaning didn't register.

"Yeah, my short-story professor, she's brilliant." The tension escaped from his face at the *she* pronoun. "I want to take another class with her. She said I could, she'd be happy to have me again. She's the one who gave me the A plus."

"Right, Professor . . ."

"Caldwell."

He finished his glass of champagne. "What's so brilliant about her?"

"Like, the things she had us read? They were just so interesting. *Dubliners* is so good! I mean, 'Araby' is just heartbreaking, how could you not want to cry at the end when he's waiting for her? I'm understanding things about literature I never even knew I didn't know."

He snorted. "You're acting like I haven't taught you anything."

"What are you talking about?"

He grabbed a bowl from the cupboard, we planned ice cream to end the meal, and the cabinet door hit the wood. "Ever since you left it's like you forgot everything—everything. How many nights did I stay up late with you at that stupid diner? Things you'd never read, you couldn't even appreciate them before me. You didn't even try."

I wasn't so drunk that I couldn't now see where this was going. I realized how much more than me he'd had to drink already.

"Why don't you teach me something for once, Ali? Why don't you do the work?"

I knew it was a trap, but I didn't know what else to do. I stared at my half-empty drink. "Could you pour me another?" I tried to do my sexy smile, the uptalk I knew he responded positively to.

"Fine." He grabbed my glass. "But why don't you play teacher? Show us what you've learned at Ithaca."

"Okay, so," I began, knowing he'd at least be interested in one of the authors we read. "We read all these Poe short stories, the gothic serials? Professor Caldwell talked about how that was the birth of the short story, when he published them serially, so Poe is the father of the short story. I always just thought of him as writing those creepy poems, like that 'Annabel Lee'—"

"You're wrong," he interrupted. "Poe isn't the father of the short story. I don't know what school your professor went to, but it wasn't a good one. Certainly not Cornell. Maybe she went to Ithaca College." He laughed at how funny he was.

"But we read the original pieces, the ones first published in parts *in* the newspapers, people weren't writing like that before."

"Ali, you don't even know what an idiot you sound like right now. Washington Irving was writing short stories years before Poe. *Irving* is the father of the short story." He leaned into the cushion as he sat back on the couch next to me. "You're so gullible. You listen to anyone and believe them. It's sweet, really. I know you're really smart. You're just confused right now."

He tried to touch my face as he laughed a little. I shoved his hand away. "I'm not stupid."

"I didn't call you stupid. I said you were smart. You're being misled—"

"I am not." I was up from the couch and standing in front of the TV. "Poe *was* the father of the short story. Did it ever occur to you that maybe *you're* wrong?"

"Hey—*you're* wrong. I went to Cornell. I got a degree from Columbia." He was sitting straight backed on the couch. "Who do you think knows more about English literature? A college freshman or an English teacher?"

"My college professor." I started toward the bedroom to get my backpack and things together. "I want to go home. Don't call me stupid."

He tried to get ahead of me, pulling me back. "I didn't call you stupid!" Full voice yelling now.

"Whatever!" I yelled back. "I want to go."

Something broke through in him. He started yelling, almost incoherently, piling up my things in his arms, voice booming the whole time, and I stood against the wall and waited. By now I knew I just had to wait. He took my things into the living room and pulled open his front door, he was on the second floor of the apartment building, and there was a balcony. He tossed everything into the outside air. I watched a pair of underwear float down, the *thwop* of a shoe hitting the pavement, the other clothes and a book and my bag of makeup fall and shatter the quiet. "There! Get the fuck out!"

I screamed back at him, we screamed at each other. I heard my voice rage through my throat. At some point he started to cry, on the carpet, with huge sobs racking his body. Then I started to cry. I leaned over him, apologizing, promising him this would never happen again. We made up on the living room floor. After, I put on his coat and boots and went outside into the snow, picked up my clothes and shoes one by one, making multiple trips because I couldn't carry as much, moving slowly so I didn't trip in the too-big shoes. I walked back in for the last time as the ball dropped. Nick was asleep on the couch. Dick Clark congratulated the darkness, "Happy New Year!" I shut the door to the night air and slowly refolded my clothes on the carpet.

22

We had been having the nonspecific, circular fights couples have when they're going to break up. We'd been having those for a while. It felt like everywhere I turned there was an argument, and I didn't know how to stop them anymore. Fights about where I was when he called and I didn't pick up, who I was with, why couldn't I just be patient, when could we tell people about us, how much longer would I have to lie, when would things ever change at all? We stopped saying *I love you* before we hung up the phone. We'd become a couple who screamed at each other, even if we knew others could hear us.

On a Sunday morning in January, we had breakfast at Denny's near Ithaca, where we got a 20 percent off coupon as part of our hotel stay. All of the plans for our future were falling apart—him going to grad school at Cornell seemed less and less likely. There was no chance of our "just two students in Ithaca" fantasy happening anytime soon. He still hadn't told any of his friends and family, and I wasn't allowed to tell anyone. Teenagers couldn't be trusted, he said. He had told Mr. Ulman, my theater teacher from our high school, about us, but it made me feel icky and embarrassed. And Nick acted like I should be thrilled.

I wiped my mouth with my napkin, ready to say what I'd been thinking for weeks. "I don't see a future for us."

"Let's talk about this back at the hotel," he said.

"I'd really rather you take me home," I said. The ask was pointless and I knew it. My things were still at the hotel. We were here with his car, no one even knew where I was, much less who I was with. Who could I call to pick me up, hours away from home on a snowy weekend? It was winter break, so home was my parents' house, not my dorm, even though that was much closer. Students weren't allowed back until the end of January.

"We need to get our stuff first, right?" He was too calm. I didn't even have any quarters to make a phone call. My cell phone was in my car a hundred miles away.

"Okay," I said. He paid the check, using the coupon. I put down cash for the tip.

As he shut the door behind him, his voice barreled through the hotel room. I don't remember the words, but it was all the same. I yelled things back. I tried to put my things into my backpack, he threw them against the wall. I tried to get out the door, but he had double-locked it and I wasn't fast enough. I was crying now and he had begun apologizing, begging me to stay with him, how he needed me and loved me and didn't I see how lucky we were. He pulled me away from the door and pushed me onto the bed.

I knew what was happening. I heard my underwear rip. It didn't matter. He always bought me new ones. On the bed on my back I fixed my eyes on a corner of the ceiling, the window shade still open so the winter sun spilled in. I had thrown the heavy blinds apart that morning, trying to wake him up. I had wanted coffee. No one had closed them. Now just the sheers and glass remained between me and the rest of the world. A whole other kind of world than the one I was in.

I watched his shadow move in that corner. Like shadow puppets from my childhood. *This is how you make a dog, this is how you make an alligator, a butterfly.* His looked like a monster. Attacking. I thought about what monster that shadow could be—a hydra? a cyclops? a chimera? I squeezed my eyes shut and tried to remember what we read in Latin. None of those were right. I didn't have a name for this one. I tried to be silent and still so it wouldn't notice me. I listened to the awful sounds his body in my body made. And then Nick rolled me over, and the shadows merged into one big blackness, my face against the bed, the sounds of animal noises being made in the room, the way the white linens on the mattress became more and more damp from all the salt and water my body was expelling. I could feel it with my fingers.

This wasn't some ritual I needed to survive to grow up. It was a violence.

When he was done, he pawed my breast, kissed the back of my neck, and told me he loved me.

"I love you, too."

—

After, while he napped, I watched the light die between the curtains. It was still snowing, so everything reflected itself on the snow, and it seemed brighter than it really was. We were supposed to check out hours ago, but a knock on the door never came.

I repacked our bags, and as Nick settled the bill, the hotel receptionist kept looking at me in this certain way I hadn't seen in a long time, this sort of sadness on her face, and a little surprise, like seeing a ghost. I recognized it as pity. Nick didn't seem to notice.

He drove us home in the snow, playing John Mayer on his stereo, and when our song was on, Nick sang and held and kissed my hand. The darkness opened up and swallowed the car. I listened to the lyrics, John Mayer singing to a girl about their secret relationship that no one could know about, not her friends, not her mother, but how it would become *love soon*, and I realized I didn't like that song anymore. It sounded twangy and the lyrics were singsong and dumb. I wasn't sure anymore if I ever liked it at all.

23

Something changed when I got back to campus for the spring semester. I started not waiting by the phone for him, which at first I would apologize for, for being shallow and wanting to be with other students. But the more I stopped waiting, the more I kept wanting to be with other people. I was tired of being alone. I realized our relationship had no hope of changing anytime soon. Something shifted in me, irreparable.

Things dissolved, rapidly. It's blurry and angry in my memory, but I printed out IM conversations from those first weeks of my second semester, all-caps typing back and forth over where I was when I didn't answer my phone, how he never answered his phone except when he wanted to talk, asking if he wanted me to quit school so I could be with him, cursing him and the whole relationship. Followed by fifty-four messages asking me to please take him back and forgive him.

We began breaking up and getting back together at a

rapid pace. The final message I printed out from him was from February 6:

> I wanted so badly to come up this weekend. Why I even thought about wasting 8 hours in a car and taking time off is beyond me when the girl on the other side of that drive could fucking care less if I'm there or not. A girl who doesn't love me and doesn't care about my feelings. A girl who only cares about herself and only wants to cut herself off from the people that love her. . . . I already miss you. I'm sorry I wasted any of your time. Please don't sell the ring. Someday, you may love it again, you may love me again, and you'll be sorry it's gone, you'll be sorry I'm gone. Just know that I will always love you. I will be here if you need me even though I know you'll never ask.

I broke up with him for good before Valentine's Day, over the phone. It was on a Thursday night so I knew he couldn't drive up to see me and try to convince me to change my mind. He had school the next day. He didn't get angry that time. He sort of chuckled and said, "Okay, Dinah." I could hear the incredulity in his phrasing. It felt like just another time he didn't take me seriously. I hung up without saying goodbye.

He called back. I didn't answer. He called and called again. And again. My computer chirped along, alerting me to his IMs. Over and over, *Ali. Ali. Ali. Ali, I love you. Please. Ali.* But he didn't leave a message on my answering machine.

Just called and left silence. I took the phone off the hook and clanged it onto my desk, and when the dial tone didn't stop I shoved it under my bed, the twirled wire stretching taut.

—

I woke up in the middle of that same night. I hung up my phone and closed our IM window without reading the messages. I shut my eyes and tried to release my shoulders. I said to myself, *This is what you want. This is what you wanted.*

But part of me still wished he would show up the day after, drive up out of the blue to try to win me back, make all the promises and all the apologies. That part of me still wished he would make a wild romantic gesture and that we didn't have to hide anymore and that I was worth more than any job.

My phone didn't ring the next day.

—

A friend of a friend liked me, and he asked me out that weekend. His name was Henry. I knew him from a class, a boy I met a few times prior and talked to over keg beers, under string lights, at some party—one of the few nights I wasn't waiting by the phone. He was nice. Young. My age. He had a radio show on campus, which I thought was cool. I said yes to the date. I didn't want to be half a person anymore in college. I didn't want to pretend to have headaches and listen to the other girls in my hall talk about how fun the night before was and have nothing to add to the conversation. They had stopped inviting me to go out. What was the point? I always bailed. I had a secret boyfriend I didn't talk about. They knew I was hiding something and had lost interest in figuring out what it was. I couldn't blame them.

Henry and I saw *Daredevil* on Valentine's Day together, and it was a terrible movie, but when he kissed me good night in front of my dorm, it wasn't terrible. He had put his arm around me in the dark theater, finally, after multiple stops and starts to get closer. After the movie, we had laughed over sodas at a late-night diner at how truly bad the acting was. He wore a black hoodie and a band T-shirt. He barely had a beard. He was nineteen years old. Just like me.

I was supposed to be in a hotel with Nick that night. A fancy one, the cutest inn in town. He kept putting off making the reservation, though, and in the end I wasn't sure if he ever had. I couldn't make the reservation myself. I didn't have a credit card.

Throughout the week, a handful of cards and letters were delivered from Nick. I didn't open them. Words weren't enough anymore; they had lost their hold on me. I wasn't even angry about it. I was bored.

In the book, especially in part two, Lolita is repeatedly, unflatteringly, described as bored. *A most exasperating brat . . . her fits of disorganized boredom.* I remember reading that in high school and rolling my eyes at those parts, as I had already begun to be bored by the book myself. Of *course* she's over it. Of course she ends up leaving. It annoyed me to no end how Nick insisted I was misreading, how beautiful all of that was, and how she was just acting out.

I realized that maybe I wasn't the one misreading the situation. I was tired of being alone to hide our relationship. I was tired of protecting Nick by isolating myself. My life had been so empty. I was missing everything. I was as bored as Lolita was. And if Lolita could make another choice, a choice to leave, so could I. I was ready to choose something else.

24

Eventually, I did open the letters. They were all apologies and proclamations of love. The exact things I had so desperately wished to hear for so long. One was a four-page letter, listing fifty things he was sorry for and twenty things he was not sorry for.

1. *I'm sorry for ever yelling.*
2. *I'm sorry for making you feel like I might hit you.*
3. *I'm sorry I don't always listen.*
4. *I'm sorry I don't let you finish what you are saying.*
5. *I'm sorry for the times you didn't come.*
6. *I'm sorry I don't let you speak your mind.*
7. *I'm sorry I wasn't there for you last semester.*
8. *I'm sorry I couldn't fix this.*
9. *I'm sorry I don't know what's wrong with us.*
10. *I'm sorry I was ever "fat."*

11. *I'm sorry I waste your time.*

12. *I'm sorry I go on and on and on when I talk.*

13. *I'm sorry if I seem like a know-it-all.*

14. *I'm sorry I'm a burden.*

15. *I'm sorry if you missed out on anything this year because of me.*

16. *I'm sorry you think I'm too old.*

17. *I'm sorry I embarrass you.*

18. *I'm sorry if I ask for too much.*

19. *I'm sorry if you ever felt like you weren't enough.*

20. *I'm sorry I'm so far away.*

21. *I'm sorry I'm not there now.*

22. *I'm sorry I ever doubted you.*

23. *I'm sorry this relationship didn't seem real to you.*

24. *I'm sorry you had to wait for me.*

25. *I'm sorry we couldn't tell anyone.*

26. *I'm sorry I didn't see your side of things sooner.*

27. *I'm sorry I just finally told people and didn't do it sooner.*

28. *I'm sorry I can't ever say the right thing.*

29. *I'm sorry I can't ever do the right thing.*

30. *I'm sorry I can't take your pain away.*

31. *I'm sorry I never answer my phone.*

32. *I'm sorry I'm a computer moron.*

33. *I'm sorry I was ever condescending.*

34. *I'm sorry if I ever made you feel inferior.*

35. *I'm sorry for when I didn't respect your opinion.*

36. *I'm sorry I make you angry.*

37. *I'm sorry I ever made you cry.*
38. *I'm sorry I don't like foreign films or keep old notes & things.*
39. *I'm sorry if you weren't always convinced that I loved you.*
40. *I'm sorry I ruin conversations with my "Stupid Mouth."*
41. *I'm sorry I made you feel like I didn't want you to have fun.*
42. *I'm sorry I made you feel like I didn't want you to meet people.*
43. *I'm sorry about my ego.*
44. *I'm sorry if I ever made money an issue.*
45. *I'm sorry that I can't always understand you.*
46. *I'm sorry if I ever made you think you're high maintenance you're not.*
47. *I'm sorry if I ever thought you didn't love me.*
48. *I'm sorry I ever disappointed you.*
49. *I'm sorry this has come to this.*
50. *I'm sorry I'm not the fantasy you had.*
    —But I'm not sorry, also:
1. *I'm not sorry we met.*
2. *I'm not sorry about the night @ Star Wars.*
3. *I'm not sorry for "not" on the first night.*
4. *I'm not sorry I like sushi.*
5. *I'm not sorry I got you the ring.*
6. *I'm not sorry we spent the summer and holidays together.*
7. *I'm not sorry about ever going to Rhapsody.*

8. *I'm not sorry for one moment we have shared to-gether.*

9. *I'm not sorry for ever driving to I.C.*

10. *I'm not sorry you're not older.*

11. *I'm not sorry you are you.*

12. *I'm not sorry I saw John Mayer.*

13. *I'm not sorry that I write songs for you.*

14. *I'm not sorry we talked about our future together.*

15. *I'm not sorry I told Gabe.*

16. *I'm not sorry I told Lisa.*

17. *I'm not sorry I told Ulman.*

18. *I'm not sorry for making love to you.*

19. *I'm not sorry for kissing you.*

20. *I'm not sorry that I love you.*

He ended it writing:

Alisson, I could go on forever. I had something completely different written for you until we spoke on Thursday and you told me your decision. . . . What I really do know is that I think of you right now and I get that same sick anticipation and excitement and goose bumps that I got when I looked at you a year ago. . . . I folded and refolded the letter.

Nick kept calling, even after I told him I was dating someone else, and he kept sending letters. I stopped keeping them.

I started going out on weekend nights with the girls from my hall. With my new boyfriend. We stayed out all night drinking and laughing. Henry took me to the art house cinema across town at Cornell to see black-and-white movies or weird cult films. We hung out in big groups of people, with his hand in mine, his arm around me. We went bowling. We took photos together. I tacked them onto my walls for anyone to see. But I didn't tell him, or anyone, about the teacher. Even though it was over, and the sharp sadness that would hit my stomach if something reminded me of Nick faded every day, the fact that I had a secret stayed. And stayed. And somehow felt heavier as the days went on. Or maybe I began noticing it more because there wasn't anything happy or exciting about keeping the secret to distract me. Now, the secret wasn't anything else but lies.

—

Over spring break, back in my childhood bedroom, I couldn't sleep. I was so close to Nick, only thirty minutes away instead of five hours. I knew he would never show up at my parents' house, but I couldn't shake this feeling—like I was trapped. Like he had some hold over me. I decided I wanted to take everything back. There were a lot of mementos from the past year and a half he had kept, that he didn't let me bring to college. Notes from when I was still a high school student, a journal we wrote back and forth in. And I still had his apartment key.

Even though I was on break, I knew public schools weren't. I drove to his apartment in the middle of the day and let myself in. I sat next to his cat, Duchess, on his couch, she finally liked me enough to let me pet her, until she hissed at me and walked away. She was hard to read. I went to his bedroom, saw the sheets tangled, and made the bed for him. I slowly smoothed the fold over the quilt, both hands running across the cotton. The sheets were so white. The coverlet was burgundy. The two colors against each other, that first morning when I bled and he screamed at me. I fluffed the pillows.

In the corner of the room was a small wooden cabinet. I knew everything from us was in the bottom drawer. I opened it.

It smelled like my perfume. All the photographs of us, well, of each of us back-to-back. The accompanying negatives. Notes on lined paper. Happy Meal toys we got during road trips that he kept. Receipts from hotels.

I took a pillowcase from his linen closet and shoved the things inside, not caring if photo edges were being bent or if paper was ripping. I didn't know why I was crying or when I started. I realized when I saw drops darken the paper in my hands. I petted Duchess one more time. I left his key on his bedside table and locked the door behind me. I didn't write a note.

—

When I got back to college after spring break, to the friends I was making, to my new boyfriend, I still felt this hollow feeling rattling around inside. The closer I got to people, the worse I felt about skating around my past, not explaining things.

I needed to tell someone. I decided to talk to Richie, who knew Nick from the school plays. His dorm was only a few minutes away from me on campus, and he was one of the reasons Nick and I had to be so secretive, even here. Richie and I sat on a bench outside in the cold and I told him I had to tell him something.

I don't remember exactly what I said. I don't remember much of Richie's reaction. I just remember this lift inside, like every word was something leaving. I told him the whole story—meeting at the diner, the code on the chalkboard, sleeping with Mr. North after graduation, road trips, how we had just been in Ithaca together a month ago. I showed him the Tiffany ring. I was wearing it. I didn't know why. I remember Richie believed me and promised he wouldn't tell anyone else. And I remember what it felt like to tell someone—to open my hand and let the secret fly away. How free.

25

Even after telling Richie, I wanted it all to be gone. I wanted it to have never happened. In my dorm room, I put the ring in the same box where I kept all of Nick's letters, the hall passes collected that year in high school, and the things I had taken back—a tie of his, the few notes from school he never knew I had, photographs—and shoved it under the bed. But *Lolita* stayed on my shelf. I hated it. It wasn't enough to hide it away, I wanted it to disappear. I wanted to burn it.

It was a snowstorm, late. Even though it was spring, there was still snow, it was upstate New York, after all. I had a nightgown on and a parka, my winter boots. It wasn't the perfect time, but once the idea sparked I couldn't let it go. I took matches from my desk drawer, Nick's forgotten matches, for his cigarettes, and tramped into the darkness. I knew I would have to go far enough into the woods behind the dorm that no one would see and call campus security. The moon made everything glow. I held the book in my mitten, the matches in my pocket. I chose a spot and bent down, pushed snow away so there was a resting place for *Lolita*, for fire to meet paper.

I imagined the book would alight in flame, the pages would dance as they transformed into ash, that this burning would free me from the teacher and absolve me from all of my lies. It would be a cleansing fire, the kind in myths, the kind witches conjured to break spells—the cover would morph from *Lolita/Nabokov* to black smoke and my heart would be free. A perfect ending to all of it.

The book simply smoldered. I pushed the snow farther away from the pages as the flames licked them, but everything was too cold and frozen, the surrounding ice only continued to melt in a cycle of firefighting, *Lolita* lying there, pathetic and dead.

I stood in my nightgown and parka in the night and watched, too tired from everything to feel any fire inside me anymore. I just wanted this effigy to work. For the end to be as dramatic as the entire relationship was—what better way to show the very gods of literature that I was *so* over this fauxwriter-teacher-lover than by burning the book he used to seduce me in the first place? The very book that was supposed to be "us," bursting into flames.

It felt like everything I wanted was not meant to be. I stamped on the book, kicked snow over the flame-gummed edges. Another failure. Just like us. Just like Lolita and Humbert even, she didn't make it to the end of the novel, and he ends up dead too. It was over for all of us—Humbert, Lolita, Nick, and me.

I began trudging back to my dorm, the streetlight in the distance reflecting off the snowdrifts. I kept turning back hoping the book would have lit itself somehow, magically, and that it would be a sign that it was all for a reason, that this would be meaningful somehow. Any affection I had had for the book had emptied along with my affection for Nick, Mr. North, my teacher. What an obvious, dumb story. It's not even interesting. Boy meets girl, girl seduces boy, they run away, and everyone ends up dead. At the edge of the trees, I looked back once more. Only darkness. And I wondered— what would have happened to Lolita if she'd survived?

part iii

dissection

There is no part three in *Lolita*. Nabokov ends with everyone dead: Charlotte, Quilty, Humbert, and, of course, Lolita. A Shakespearean tragedy with less visible blood onstage. While a certain Russian author might roll in his grave at the break with his borrowed literary structure, this story goes on. I didn't die. While the mirror between *Lolita* and my life ends here, the images continued to warp and multiply. And so, without a book to guide me anymore, I went on.

1

A year later, *Lolita* broke my heart. I was now a sophomore in college, still lost in the last fits of my breakup with the teacher. My friends tried to be supportive but couldn't understand why I was so upset—"He was a guy from your high school. What was the big deal?" Neither Henry nor the girls I now considered my closest friends knew the truth.

I signed up for Psychoanalysis of Literature, as part of my English / creative writing double major. It was with my favorite professor, the same one Nick had mocked over a year ago. As the course progressed, the relationship with Nick continued to echo in my world even though it was entirely over, the noise drowning out my studies. Then *Lolita* was assigned. I skimmed the book since I had read it before, most of it, at least, and went to class feeling prepared to discuss the provocative prose, the metaphoric meaning of Lepidoptera, and the allure of forbidden love.

Professor Caldwell started class by writing, *Who's seduc-*

ing whom? on the blackboard. She wore a black T-shirt and jeans, more casual than any of my high school teachers were allowed to be. I stayed quiet, even though I knew the answer: *Lolita, of course. Humbert couldn't make that any clearer. I mean, he says it plainly and repeatedly.* Unless my professor was referring to Nabokov seducing the reader with language? I waited for the right moment to raise my hand. I had already learned this. I wasn't even taking notes. But the conversation shifted.

I remember the moment my professor referred to Humbert Humbert as an "unreliable narrator." The phrase rang through my mind. I wrote it down in my notebook. Underlined it. Then circled. I felt my spine straighten and something invisible creep down my neck.

She went on, describing Dolores Haze—I noticed Professor Caldwell made a point to call her by her real name, not Lolita—as a teenage girl who was easily groomed for abuse. "If you let a teenage girl eat whatever she wanted, she would eat pizza every day. But she would die of scurvy. Teenagers aren't equipped to make the best choices for themselves," she continued. "*Lolita* isn't a story about love, factually, it's a story about rape and obsession."

If my heart were a butterfly, her lecture plucked it bare, wing by wing.

I stayed to meet with Professor Caldwell after class, to try and understand. I began talking about love and the beauty of Nabokov's word choices, and she gently corrected me. "It's Nabokov."

"What?"

"You're saying Nah-bah-koff. It's Nah-*bow*-kov."

I felt shame race through my skin. Nick didn't even know how to pronounce Nabokov's name. And I never even questioned his authority, his understanding of the words, of the story. That he could possibly be wrong.

I walked back to my dorm through campus in a daze, the wind reaching my neck through my scarf. Intellectually, I had known by the end that my relationship with Nick was problematic and unhealthy; I mean, I had broken up with him. He had become a total jerk. But still, we were in love. He loved me, he told me so. Even if it didn't work out between us, our story, our *Lolita*, was a love story. It had to be.

—

After Professor Caldwell's lecture, I began rereading *Lolita*, the idea of Humbert as an unreliable narrator fixed in my mind. I wasn't even familiar with that term before her class. My bedside lamp shone brightly as I turned the pages all night. Today, I would argue that Humbert is a predator from page one. But, back then, I had to reread all the way to the end of part one for things to fall into place inside me. The last chapter of part one of *Lolita*, chapter 33, is Humbert basically listing the presents he bought Dolores the morning after they first have intercourse, after he informs her that her mother is dead, the very sexiest of seductions. In the middle of the paragraph-long catalog of items, including comic books, a box of candy, nail polish, sodas, tucked in the middle of all these girl-child baubles is *a box of sanitary pads*. A box of menstrual pads? I underlined this too. Did she spontaneously get her period? Was this a moment of paternal care?

And then Nick's face flashed in front of me, the cold water and anger when he looked at the sheets the morning after we first had sex. *She was bleeding from the sex. Like I did.* Because Humbert wasn't exactly gentle. And he knew he hurt her, which he hid within the text so that readers wouldn't notice it. But it was there for a purpose: to manipulate the readers. To convince them that Humbert Humbert was honest, true, even vulnerable in his telling of the story. Almost like saying, *But I told you, dear reader. It was right there.* As if it were enough to acknowledge the violence in his sex with Dolores only by implying it in the midst of a rattled-off, seemingly insignificant list.

I thought of another long list. I still kept everything from the teacher, from Nick, in a box under my bed. My mind went to one of the letters he sent me after I broke up with him, the one asking me to reconsider my decision, when he listed page after page of things he was sorry for—in the end fifty things he *was* sorry for (*1. I'm sorry for ever yelling; 2. I'm sorry for making you feel like I might hit you; 3. I'm sorry I don't always listen*), along with another twenty things he was *not* sorry for (*18. I'm not sorry for making love to you; 19. I'm not sorry for kissing you; 20. I'm not sorry that I love you*). Lost in the middle of these lists, underneath and above proclamations of never-ending love, were acknowledgments that our relationship was built on lies, that he physically threatened me and was verbally abusive, that he isolated me in high school and continued to while I was at college, none of which actually sounds anything like love (*33. I'm sorry I was ever condescending; 34. I'm sorry if I ever made you feel inferior*).

I thought of how Nabokov used Edgar Allan Poe's poetry in *Lolita*, even naming Humbert's first love, the mold for all his future nymphets in the book, Annabel, after the titular lost love of Poe's famous poem "Annabel Lee." Not coincidentally, Poe had married his thirteen-year-old cousin, Virginia. In Humbert's purported diary, the novel *Lolita*, he writes of other high-art literati who engaged with girls in nymphatic ways: Dante loved his Beatrice at nine years old, Petrarch was infatuated with a girl of twelve. That kind of referential work romanticized and aggrandized Humbert's predilection for nymphets, making it seem not only normal but aspirational.

Like how Nick then used Nabokov, his fancy prose style in *Lolita*, with me. They were both leveraging poetry in their storytelling, the power of allusions to other heralded male authors, to intimidate and persuade their audience of their version of things. Using language to convince the reader, to convince me, that they were smarter and knew what was best. That what was good enough for Edgar Allan Poe, for Nabokov, for Nick, should be more than good enough for me. That a pedophiliac-inspired, inappropriate lust was the highest form of romance. *10. I'm not sorry you're not older.*

—

That moment of understanding *Lolita*, a year after my relationship with Nick ended, is crystallized within my memory. Even then I wanted desperately to reach through time and space back to myself at seventeen and twist my skin until I stopped and listened to what the me of a year later had learned: *That is not love. Do not get caught.* But that's not how knowledge works. These were things I would have to learn as a seventeen- and eighteen-year-old, how secrets aren't a code for love. How words can dissolve and distort.

Even then, *Lolita* taught me the power of words. The allure of the poetic devices on the page entices the reader, the repetition of Ls in that opening chapter, the way an L sounds in your mouth, how Nabokov tells you the movement of your tongue when you say it, word by word: Lolita. Language. Love. As Nabokov said, in a *Playboy* interview: "One of the most limpid and luminous letters is L. The suffix '-ita' has a lot of Latin tenderness. . . . Hence: Lolita." It was all intentional. How repetition creates patterns that innately link things together.

I wanted to believe that Nick's patterns—of manipulating and misleading me, of making me feel small and stupid—were unconscious, an accident. That Nick didn't mean to damage me the way that he did, in a way I didn't recognize until much later. That he really did love me. The constant woe-is-me of the narrator in *Lolita*, and Nick in our relationship, was an emotional roller coaster that whipped me in. Nick was continuously apologizing, then implicating me and my own understanding of our relationship in the lies and deceit. *Didn't I see how much he was hurting for me?* Not unlike how Nabokov links his Humbert to Christ himself in the final line of the opening chapter: *Look at this tangle of thorns.*

Nick modeled our so-called love after *Lolita*. That was what he constantly compared us to, what he longed for us to be. I knew from Professor Caldwell's lecture that Nabokov had created Humbert as a monster on purpose, that in his own words, "Humbert Humbert is a vain and cruel wretch who manages to appear 'touching.'" Humbert abuses and controls Dolores, doesn't even allow her to have her own name, an identity outside of his lust. How did Nick not see that?

I wrote my final paper for class, "Some Girls Have Everything: Lolita and Blame," about how the novel sets up Dolores as the cause of her own doom, the curves in the language that set up the skewed perspective so the readers don't understand the manipulation happening in front of them. It's clear my understanding of the situation at that time, on the page and in my life, was only in words. I wrote, "Yet what young girl would not be flushed and pleased to know that a handsome, older man fancied her?" I got an A plus, with Professor Caldwell noting at the end, "Sad, but sharp and accurate."

I understood for the first time, I saw that maybe I was the one who misread our relationship and *Lolita*. Maybe I had been the unreliable narrator in our story. Maybe I was a lot like Lolita after all.

2

Three years after the relationship ended, I was visiting an apple orchard with a friend, reaching from a wooden ladder into the branches. Leaves in my hair, the Ithaca sky clear and blue above me. There was an apple in my hand, the heavy, cool firmness. The skin was mottled green transforming into red, matte and smooth. I pulled and the stem tensed and broke from the branch with a snap and I was suddenly struck with desire (apple, lightning): I wanted to see him. I had a vision of the scene in *Lolita* where Humbert throws her an apple, and shame pitted into my stomach. It was a weekend, I had a full tank of gas in my car and no work on Monday at the bar where I was waitressing. I had no specific or clear motivation, but I was twenty-two and impulsive. I needed to see Nick's face. I started to drive.

I showed up at his apartment unannounced, my only passenger a bag full of apples. It was dark now. I didn't know why I was there, why I had driven five hours to see him without an invitation. Outside of the threshold to his apartment, I saw a line of shoes, including a pair of small heels. I saw them but didn't make the logical jump in the moment—he wasn't alone. I knocked on the door and felt my body snap back when a girl answered. She was young and blond. A freshman in college, maybe? Younger than me. I didn't recognize her. She called out to Nick and there he was, looking at me again.

Nick and I sat on his porch and talked for a long time. I don't remember what we said—I'm sure it was the *how have you been* formalities of catch-up. I didn't know how to start the conversation that had been circling in my skull the whole drive. I tried to bring up *us*. In response, he waxed on about how lucky I was to have him in my life when I did. What a gift he was to me, to have someone older and wiser at such a crucial moment in a young girl's life. I just listened. I remember thinking he had gained weight. That his hairline had begun to creep away from his brow. I remember once he elbowed me in the arm playfully, that electric connection still there. It shocked me.

At one point, he asked me if I wanted a drink. "I could make you a cosmo . . . ?" A vague hand gesture to his apartment behind him.

"I drink whiskey now," I said. "Are you still drinking Humberts?"

He gazed into the dark parking lot in response. There wasn't anything to see. He changed the subject.

We sat and talked for so long that the blond girl came outside. "So, I'm going to get going. . . ." Nick hadn't given her any explanation of who I was or why I was there.

I stood up—"No, no, I have to go. I'm so sorry for interrupting"—before Nick could choose who he wanted to stay. I didn't want to know.

I had so much I still wanted to say, that I wanted to ask him—Did he really love me then? Was I really special? Why did he think what happened was okay? I wasn't brave enough. I was afraid of all the possible answers, I was afraid of them and what they would mean, not to mention his potentially explosive reaction if I pushed too hard or said the wrong thing. So I gave Nick an apple, kissed him on the cheek, and told them both goodbye.

3

The last time I saw Nick was after I was raped by my boss at work. I was twenty-three. I was a wreck, deeply frightened by what had happened to me, flooded daily with PTSD symptoms. The criminal case went nowhere, I was trying to put together a new life. I felt unmoored and in danger of losing everything.

I sent Nick an email out of the blue, asking him to get a coffee sometime, promising it wasn't to have *a big talk or anything . . . hope that's not too frightening*. He emailed me back less than a day later with his cell phone number.

I felt as though no one knew me anymore. In my new apartment, a few miles away from my hometown, I drove back and forth to an internship. I never cooked. I watched old movies, the sweeping black-and-white romances starring Rita Hayworth, Fred Astaire, Ginger Rogers, Humphrey Bogart. Those were the only stories I wanted. I bought cat food for my cats. I didn't go out much. Who was there to go out with? Most of my friends had moved on after finishing college. The last time I had felt this separate from my life, I was a senior in high school. It all felt unsettlingly familiar. Nick was my instinctual reach.

A few years after Dolores escaped Humbert in *Lolita*, she sends him a letter. It is a cry for help. She is in trouble, pregnant, in debt. She needs him.

In *Lolita*, Humbert shows up. Money in hand and an offer to take her away from all this. She declines the offer but takes the check. This time, he respects her choice. She ends up dead, anyway.

—

Nick and I got lunch. It was warm out, so we were outside, at a cute restaurant on the water. Not a diner at all. He wore sunglasses he kept taking on and off, removing them for effect when he wanted to look into my eyes, to underscore something he was saying. I looked and looked at him. He looked the same. Same short-brimmed hat, same green eyes, a little more weight on his stomach. But something felt off. Maybe it was all the sunshine instead of fluorescent lights. Maybe it was sitting openly in a restaurant in our hometown. Maybe it was how empty my body felt when he hugged me *hello*.

He was so happy to see me. He told me he still loved me, sunglasses off. I told him what had happened. He put his sunglasses back on, told me he was so sorry, what could he do? Anything I needed. *Anything*.

He was dating someone else. Sunglasses off, pushing his hair back so I could see his ever-receding hairline. He dropped his voice, as if someone could overhear—he "didn't have a girlfriend, but wasn't exactly single." He asked me if I wanted to come over later that night, it was basically over with her anyway, and he could tell I needed him now. Another offer of secrets.

I demurred and suggested he call me when it was definitely over. Sunglasses back on. He kissed me goodbye and promised it would be soon. He had missed me *so much*.

Over a month later, I sent him a long email, subject line *so*. It clearly wasn't over with her, whoever she was. I told him I needed him as a friend—*i just need someone to talk to and for some reason i want it to be you*.

I wanted him to save me again. I was in trouble, and that was what I had been taught—I needed him to make it through. It didn't even make sense then, and somewhere I knew that, but nothing was making sense in my life. I was trying what had worked, at least for a little while, before.

He never emailed me back. We haven't spoken since, over ten years ago.

4

Throughout the rest of my twenties, I worked with teenagers at a series of nonprofit organizations. I ran leadership groups after school for teen girls, I taught sex education in public high schools, I led a prevention program designed to help teens "choose healthy relationships" and prevent teen domestic violence. I wrote grants to fund the work I was doing, with paragraphs like these: *Evidence shows that prior victimization is the number one predictor of future victimization; that abusive relationships are cyclic in nature and victims can become trapped in a cycle of abuse that reaches through multiple partnerships. By giving teenagers the tools to make healthy relationship choices while they are still in high school, we are giving them a strong start for the rest of their lives.*

I could see, in my mid- to late twenties, how these were all tools that I wish I'd had access to when I was a teenager. And yet they were just flashes of insight I caught in my hands, cupped in my palm like lightning bugs. I did not think much of how the teacher fit into this narrative. Mr. North was not really part of my story, as I told it to myself. *Sure, it was totally fucked up*, I could say, *but it wasn't rape. I wanted it as much as he did. It was never* abuse *abuse.*

At this point, I had not read Nabokov in years. Whatever clarity I had captured in my college literature course had been let go in favor of the present, the work I was trying to do with young women, the unsuccessful attempts at healthy, romantic relationships with men in my own life. There was only so much I could hold at once. I didn't name what had happened to me then. I just let it go.

5

I began to question my memory, my very self. I was surrounded by teenage girls in my job, seeing every day how
they were decidedly *not* adults. But my idea of who I was as
a teenager was so different—I wanted to see myself clearly. I
wanted to find the photograph of me, taken that night, back-
stage, from the play. The way I felt looking at him, the power
of my gaze, how seductive I was trying to be. I remembered
the blue-and-white dress that was rented for my costume, the
brown shoes I wore that were my own. I remembered red
lipstick. I remembered looking right at the teacher when the
photo was snapped.

After days of prowling through albums and in boxes, it
appeared: and it wasn't what I remembered at all. Yes, my
mouth was red, my dress was blue and white, and my shoes
were brown leather. But my expression—there was nothing
sexy there. No power at all. I was sitting on a metal folding
chair, no one else in the frame, my chin up toward something

above me, my arms on my lap, and I didn't look like the mature woman I imagined myself to be. Pretty, yes, but more than anything, I looked sad.

Part of me wanted proof that I was asking for it, that I did look like a grown-up, maybe, that I did have some power. Deeply, I wanted to have evidence of my longing, my unmissable lust, evidence that I had agency then. That maybe I really was special and just so sexy that he *couldn't* say no, that I did seduce him after all.

Instead, I was faced with my deepest fear. I looked and looked at her. At myself. At seventeen. My eyes were big and my face open. My mouth downturned, tight. I looked as though I could be on the verge of tears. I was a child, and he wasn't. That photograph caught me at one of the moments when I remember feeling the most sexy and seductive for the teacher. And if that was even close to capturing what I really was then, any excuses I try to make for the teacher break and shatter. *Look at this tangle of thorns.*

6

A rainy October evening at the Boys & Girls Clubs of America. I was twenty-nine. Another female staff member named Stephanie and I had been leading a weekly girls-only comprehensive sex education and leadership program for more than two months, covering it all: how to put on a condom, HIV and STI information, how to negotiate safe sex and no sex, the works. We had the same eight high school girls for three hours one night a week. We always started with pizza.

We had just wrapped the official curriculum for the night. Girls were still hanging around, eating leftovers while Stephanie and I cleaned up and answered questions one-on-one when requested. Someone had spilled soda and I was wiping down the dark, hard plastic table, dark so it wouldn't show stains, while three of the oldest girls chattered. They were all seniors, seventeen and eighteen years old. Most of the girls in the group were shy at first, blushing constantly the first few weeks, but now we were all comfortable using anatomically correct words in conversation, in this room with each other, at least.

One of the girls, Nicole, who I knew had a slightly older boyfriend, was asking another girl, Liz, what her plans were this weekend. "You going out with him again?" Liz shook her head, her cheeks spotted with acne. "Nah. He's crazy." Nicole looked up from her pizza slice with her sparkly-purple-lined eyes. Liz fake-whispered, *You know.* The third girl, who until now had been silent, giggled along, snapping her gum as punctuation.

Nicole pushed her lips against her teeth. "Oh, it's like that?" They all laughed. They knew that I was right there, listening to their coded conversation, but pretended to not see me. "You know how it is!" Liz said as they elbowed each other and stuffed their mouths. Nicole flipped her hair behind her shoulder and cocked her head, saying, "Girl, it's no big deal. I've had sex with three guys. Just relax and have a good time." She took a sip of soda from a clear plastic cup, leaving a stain of bright pink on the rim. "And if you're not having a good time, it's your problem, because you gotta ask for what you want." The third girl raised her hands in agreement and clapped, "Yes!"

The girls' laughter. On the one hand, I was thrilled they were talking about sex without any accompanying shame. That was one of the goals. Slut shaming serves no one. But as I watched them zip up their raincoats and sling pastel backpacks over their shoulders, taking turns to call their parents to come pick them up on the phone at the desk, I did not see mature, sophisticated, powerful women. I saw high school students. For all her bravado, Nicole was a child. And it took everything I had in me to not grab their hands and tell them to wait, *wait*, that there was no rush in any of this, life was so long ahead of you. I wanted to tell them to stop running away from being exactly who they were—I wanted to tell them all of the things, everything. *Please stop pretending you are grown-ups*, I wanted to say.

The rain had morphed into a thunderstorm, kicking in with a flash and a crack, and the girls grabbed at each other and screamed and laughed. None of them had remembered their umbrellas. They went off into the parking lot in pairs and singles, rain reflecting off their parents' headlights, running through puddles and slamming doors. Soon it was just Nicole and me left, her mom was usually late, and I told Stephanie that I was happy to finish up, that she could go home. Nicole helped me pack up all the extra handouts, pencils, the bowl of condoms we always had out. I saw her grab a handful, push them into the pocket of her lavender slicker. She smiled at me and said, "Thank you, Miss Alisson," when I offered her candy for helping me clean up.

As she unwrapped the lollipop's waxed paper, I saw her just as she was: a seventeen-year-old girl. Not even coltish in her limbs, more fawn—all big eyes and spots from freckles and pimples and downy skin. Long eyelashes, like wings. *No one could possibly think she was a grown-up*, I thought. She picked at the edges of her nails as she waited on the other side of the front desk. A car honked, she was off and waving at me through the rain. I locked up the building, shook off my umbrella pointlessly as I got into my car, and rested my wet forehead against the steering wheel. I *was a child and* she *was a child*, the line from Poe's poem "Annabel Lee" began to unravel inside me, and I heard Mr. North's voice, how he always read things aloud to me. *In a princedom by the sea . . . these miserable memories . . . that impact of passionate recognition*, now lines from *Lolita*.

"I was a child," I said aloud. And I swear, there was lightning.

7

I don't think things would have gone particularly well for Lolita if she had survived. In Nabokov's story, she escapes her rapist, kidnapper stepfather, Humbert, for the dangerous charms of Quilty, which rhymes with guilty—Nabokov never missed a chance for wordplay. Quilty is just as wretched to Dolores as Humbert was, and he wants her to do pornos. She refuses, and he kicks her out onto the street. She is not even seventeen at this point.

The first time I read the book, I didn't realize she ended up dead until the teacher mentioned it. Upon rereading the book, I realized that it is perfectly clear—the fact that she's dead and why I missed it. She is simply defined as such in the "Foreword" of the book, purportedly written by a preeminent psychiatrist, but there she is identified only as Mrs. Richard F. Schiller, her future husband's name. Not even by Dolores, which many readers forget is her actual name anyway. No reader knows going into the book who Richard F. Schiller

is, and Lolita is not referenced by that new name until nearly
the end. Who is expected to remember that?

In the penultimate chapter, while Humbert writes, *I wish
this memoir to be published only when Lolita is no longer alive*, a
cynical reader knows that wishes do not always come true.
I assumed I had missed that detail in my sloppy skimming
and asked the teacher about this—if this is a beautiful story
about love and a story about us, I end up dead? He told me
Lolita died only because she left Humbert, that she had to
suffer a consequence for her betrayal, that's how great literature works. Bad girls end up dead. And they deserve it.

When he told me that, it wasn't as ominous as it looks
written down. He said it playfully, I laughed, as if I would
ever do anything such as betray him or cheat on him. Bad
girls get what's coming to them. And I saw Lolita as a decidedly bad girl.

—

Now when I think about the first ten years of my life after the
teacher, I see a clear impact. He was a mold in how I understood romance. I thought it was supposed to hurt. I felt safe
when I was a secret. All of that felt familiar. I found myself
unconsciously seeking out or at least choosing relationships
where I was a secret—illicit affairs, married men, guys who
just couldn't commit to even being called my "boyfriend."
The pattern made itself known. I kept thinking I was un-
lucky, that I was being lied to (and sometimes I was), that it
wasn't my fault. Deeper, I was afraid I was broken, that this
was all I could ever know in a relationship. That I was a bad

girl, too, that this was what I deserved, even wanted. It was what I was taught, about myself, about love.

I finally saw what was happening. It was after I had made the leap and moved to New York City, starting the M.F.A. program at NYU. That summer I went to a writers' conference in Oregon, sleeping in a dorm room and going to crafts talks and readings and workshops every day. I was so happy. But on the first day of the workshop, a boy sat next to me and started flirting and I flirted back. He was from New York City, too, he was a good writer and knew it. I was smitten. I kept flirting even when he was coy about his life outside of the workshop, even when I realized he was living with a girlfriend, having overheard him speak about her to someone else. *Maybe it's an open relationship,* I told myself. *Maybe they have an agreement for things like this.*

I let him buy me glasses of rosé and spin me on the dance floor at night. I took his hand back to his dorm room. I felt young, naïve, even though college and high school were more than ten years past. I let it all happen. And the next evening, after he told me he was planning on proposing to his girlfriend after he got home, I ran out of his sight and sobbed.

But now I wasn't alone. I was sharing my dorm with a close girlfriend, my best friend, splitting the cost, and as I sat and cried on my twin bed, she sat and listened. It was the first time I said what scared me so much: "What is it about me that tells men that I will keep their secret? What is it about me that tells them I want this?"

My friend rubbed my back and reassured me that *he* was the asshole, and *I* deserved someone much, much better. She encouraged me to keep talking about it in therapy. She lent me a different dress so we could go back out to the party as if everything were new.

And that was the moment when the pattern began to break. I began to understand that I was making choices to get myself into these messes and that I didn't want to be unhappy anymore. Now I had to learn how to choose differently.

—

If Lolita, Dolores, had lived, I bet she would have been in a string of shitty relationships too. How can you understand what love is supposed to be if *Lolita* is the greatest love story of our century? If that is your first romance?

During a class in my M.F.A., I argued about love with another student. I had started writing about the teacher and *Lolita*, so, naturally, the subject came up during my workshop. A guy was saying that *Lolita* was about love, that because Humbert said he was in love, it was love. Even the professor agreed. I left my mouth closed for a moment. Then I said back, "Nothing about how Humbert treats Dolores is love. Words don't matter, actions do. Language isn't enough. *Lolita* isn't about love at all. And neither, really, is what happened to me."

My words hung in the air. For what felt like the first time, no one dismissed me.

8

There's power in naming things. All the great writers know this. Some take advantage more than others of the implicit suggestions a name can create in another's mind. The places Hum and Lo travel in *Lolita* include Lake Climax, Grimm Road, Insomnia Lodge, the Enchanted Hunters hotel, *Rams-* dale, I could go on. The sexual double entendres seemingly never end. By naming something, you are claiming authority: *I have the power to define you by name.* It is a noun (a name), a verb (to name), both personal and political.

Names are innately patriarchal in Western culture, as women's surnames are malleable. A girl's name changes based exclusively on her marital status, a boy's name is the same from the day he is born. Whether you like it or not, you were probably named after your father (his last name), whose name was his father's last name, whose name was his father's, and so on. The woman disappears. The man doubles and doubles. Meet Humbert Humbert, Jr. Meet Humbert Humbert III. When was the last time you knew a girl with the exact same name as her mother?

At some point after our relationship ended, I stopped thinking of him as Nick. Or even Mr. North. In my mind, he became the Teacher. He became not so much a person anymore but an action. A teacher, one who teaches. (Implied in that statement—teaches *whom*?) Now, when I think about him, it is always surprising to think his real name. His profession, his power over me, are what I remember. Saying his name feels like a surprise. I have to stop, think of him and what he would do to me with his body, and say it: Nick.

In *Lolita*, Humbert rarely calls Dolores Haze by her real name. From the opening, it is almost always Lolita or some variation on that, his private, sexual pet name for her. It is used so much that now, when we talk about the book and the girl at the heart of the story, we talk about Lolita, not Dolores. But that's not who she is at all.

We don't use just Humbert's name for her, we use his definition too. When you call someone a "Lolita," you are calling her too sexy, too tender, dangerous. A sexually precocious young girl. In reality, a "Lolita" is a victim of a sexual predator. But that's not what we are invoking when we use "Lolita" today.

I wish I had understood *Lolita* when I read it for the first time. When the teacher read it to me. I wish I had questioned him, questioned everything about us. I wish someone else in my life, another teacher, one of my parents, even a friend, had pushed against the lies I had created, that he created for me. I wish I understood what I was giving up when I let him write our story.

9

Sometimes I worry if the whole *Lolita* intertextuality is just a conceit, a clever way to elevate what happened to me, to raise it above the tawdry. I still wonder if I have just exaggerated things, if I am the unreliable narrator in this story, if I truly did seduce him, if this *Lolita* concept is just crafted to give this relationship meaning.

But then I have in my lap a thin brown folder, the stamp collection he gave me that summer. I knew it was expensive because he told me it was. It was a limited edition, rare, special. He had to track it down and go into the city to purchase it. If I search for it online now, it is being sold for almost a hundred dollars, which to me, at eighteen, might as well have been a thousand. The packet is titled *Revised Evidence: Vladimir Nabokov's Collection of Inscriptions, Annotations, Corrections, and Butterfly Descriptions*. I open the folder and the pages of stamps are pushed together from years of abandonment, from sitting so long in the box that holds all the other pieces of paper I have from the teacher. The pressure of time made them stick together, and I crack them apart slowly, page by perforated page.

This one has twenty-one black-and-white photos of Vladimir Nabokov printed on stamps, in glasses at his typewriter, then old with a limp butterfly net. He is quoted on the side, facing the wrong way from the images, *My pleasures are the most intense known to man: writing and butterfly hunting.* This page has cropped close-ups of annotated pages of his own writing; I'm not sure if any of them are *Lolita*, as the sections are so small and partial, not even full phrases.

Then a page of stamps that has eighteen of Nabokov's drawings of his butterflies, *To Vera, from V.: Colias lolita Nab.*, a butterfly washed in what is now violet, although perhaps when this was first printed it was blue or purple. A dark black body, wings outstretched with black outskirts, one black spot in each wing, the dual antennae. And on another page, the stamps are more blurry photos of butterflies in similar shades of violet and blue.

While I can tell myself that the drawings were made from love—Nabokov watched these butterflies for hours, caught and released with soft white mesh so they could survive, and drew and painted them with water and memory and care—the *photographs* are proof that, for him, love didn't always mean hearts beating. The photographed butterflies were still, fixed forever with type-labeled pins and paste. There is no way around the fact that, in his mind, his love of Lepidoptera became a reason to kill. I don't know if they suffered, the butterflies, if in their bug brains they even understand pain.

And how does one kill something so small without damaging it? It must take great skill, practice, care of its own kind. How to capture something so completely that it remains intact, or at least looks so. Both butterfly pages are similar, there is a *Colias lolita Nab.* on each. On the edge of the page of drawings, the text: *The eastern side of every minute of mine is already colored by the light of our impending meeting. All the rest is dark, boring, you-less.*

And then—an entire stamp page of *Lolita*s. Six rows of variants on the book cover, ranging from the original green to one with a girl in heart-shaped glasses sucking a lollipop. A keyhole with a smile on the other end. A naked dark-haired girl, posing for an unseen camera. On the side appears the opening lines of *Lolita*, the lines the teacher read to me across the table that made me fall in what I swore at seventeen was love: *My sin, my soul.*

I hold in my lap, in my hand, Nick's most romantic gift to me that summer, a gift of Nabokov: his butterflies and his *Lolita*. I can feel their featherlight weight, the texture of the stamp collection, the smell of its stick. I will never know if the teacher was simply naive and shallow and incapable of close reading, if he truly did believe *Lolita* was a story about love, a story about our love, and, at almost thirty, he was unable to look any further in the text. But then he went to Cornell, Columbia—how dumb could he be? How could he ignore the cruelty, the manipulation, the pain caught in the prose?

The other version of this story is also unbearable—that the teacher was a predator, that he spent our school year grooming me to be the perfect subject for abuse, that my pain was purposeful. That I was the dumb one, a simple victim, that I fell for a story told over and over again as a warning to girls, and I ignored it because I thought I was somehow special. Instead, I am a cliché.

Even in *Lolita*, Humbert hears Dolores crying in the hotel room next door, her gentle sobs. But he knows—"she had absolutely nowhere else to go."

Once, in Nick's bedroom, as he pinned my arms to his sheets with his hands, he whispered in my ear that I was a beautiful butterfly, that I was his butterfly. I held my breath and counted my heartbeats; one, two, three. I throbbed. In this memory my eyes were closed, but now I can see—I was his butterfly.

10

Fifteen years past the teacher, I bought a butterfly. I hate butterflies. Butterflies are tramp stamp tattoos, stickers on teen girls' notebooks, metaphors about transformation that are so obvious they define cliché. So it makes perfect sense that as I walked down Broadway after a writing class at my M.F.A. program, I would notice, for the first time, though I had walked that particular stretch of New York City street multiple times, a store dedicated to nature and nature art. Which, in its window, displayed butterflies.

Dead butterflies. This was not a pet store; more like a museum of fetishized skulls and fossils and Victorian paraphernalia. Where everything is for sale. I had been reading a lot of Nabokov. Not just *Lolita*, but I had wandered into his other obsessions, specifically his scientific writings on butterflies. Nabokov was well known and well respected for his Lepidoptera, he was an affiliate at both the American Museum of Natural History and Harvard University's Museum of Comparative Zoology, sometimes devoting fourteen hours a day to drawing the wings and genitals of butterflies. He noticed the name for the adolescent stage of an insect, mid-metamorphosis: a *nymph*. Later, he would merge wings and girl and desire in creating Humbert's *nymphet*. He was a man of many passions, as he put it. Now, more than fifteen years after the teacher told me he loved me, I wanted to hold Nabokov's butterfly, his object of obsession, in my hand.

The store was bright, well labeled, filled with *things*: bleached mink jaws made into earrings, beetles trapped in amber, vintage posters displaying animal skeletons. As I walked deeper into the store, a wall of butterflies opened upon me. Dozens of framed butterflies, ranging in size from a silver dollar to larger than my palm, colors from muted to truly fluorescent. A salesclerk noticed my gaze. I told her I was looking for a "Nabokov butterfly," one of his Blues, if possible. I was a writer, I just wanted to see one in person, not in a book or on my laptop screen. The salesclerk, with bleached blond hair and very dark lipstick, was thrilled to have something specific to search for; she told me people mostly go "just for the look." After a few online searches and database checks, she led me to a cabinet in the back with seven or eight drawers, each full of dead specimens for me to consider. "I think this is what you're looking for," she said as she pointed to a small, soft brown butterfly within.

I tapped the glass softly above it, as if I wanted it to notice me. I bent down to look closer. Its wings were outstretched without any hope of wind. Its body was small, fuzzy, with a dark blue cascade that traveled out into the wings, mixing with a medium brown, the bark of a young tree. There were distinctive lines in the wings like paths and two rows of spots on the outermost expanse, an edging of white all around. I saw the blues, the distinct transitions of color, the two brushed antennae, the delicacy of it all. The longer I stared the more I saw. The very butterfly from the page of Nabokov's *Pnin*. I understood his desire. I looked at the clerk. I asked how much.

It would take two to three weeks to have her ready, to have the butterfly properly custom framed. I imagine this butterfly is a girl; I have no way of knowing. Pure projection. Unlike Nabokov, I am not possessed of the intellectual curiosity for butterfly genitalia. He made great strides in the study of butterflies' sex organs. There are entire books dedicated to his butterflies.

I had assumed for some reason that one used glue to display a butterfly, but that's not how it is done at all—you use pins. The pins in her are not the same ones my mother uses to sew with. The pin in her is longer than a simple straight pin; the clerk gave me a spare one to take home, to consider. The shaft is black, the head a pearl. If you push it against your thumb, it blows back, throbs, hums a bit, like plucking a fixed piano wire beneath the wooden lid. Flexible yet firm, it also penetrates: wings, body, skin. It holds in place. The store assured me that my butterfly had already led a full life, and was I aware that many butterflies lived only a few days? That their shortest life span is when they have wings? They are ready for death at the height of their beauty. Their purpose at that point is purely sexual, to lay eggs, to multiply. And then they die.

The quickest way to kill a butterfly is with alcohol, to trap it in a jar or in an envelope, wings carefully folded closed. Rubbing alcohol, not cosmos. But first you should pinch it hard on its thorax, a technique that takes practice to perfect, to startle it in a sense. This way, she doesn't damage herself in panic—because if the wings are ruined, the whole butterfly is a loss. This way, she suffocates. Butterflies do not make sounds. They collapse into themselves, but if they are carefully kept, they can later be rehydrated, respread for display. A butterfly caught between glass panes will be beautiful forever. *Beauty plus pity, that is the closest we can get to art*, Nabokov observed.

In the book, Nabokov kills Lolita off before she can complete her life cycle. She is pregnant but dies in child-birth, along with the child. If becoming a woman, an adult, is signified by becoming a mother, Lolita never gets there. Nabokov made her a nymphet forever.

I walked home with a butterfly pin in my pocket and photos of my butterfly on my phone. I chose a simple black wooden frame to display her, nothing ostentatious to dis-tract from her innate beauty. There was a perfect space for her on the wall above my desk at home where I sit and write, a place my eyes already went when I was at a loss between words, pages. Now when I am lost my eyes find my very own Nabokov Blue in panes of glass. I can't hold her; our skin is too oily and her wings too delicate. There will always be a cold distance between us. If I tap on the glass, nothing will happen; she's dead. But maybe looking at her will make me understand.

11

As much as I loved being a student again, I wanted to be a teacher. I was lucky—my M.F.A. program gave its graduate students an opportunity to teach an introductory creative writing course to undergraduates. I spent weeks on my syllabus, subtitling my course "Powerful Women," teaching almost exclusively women and nonbinary authors to read, switching the gothic fantasy of Edgar Allan Poe for Carmen Maria Machado, using *The Hunger Games* to teach the hero's journey instead of a Dickens novel. Instead of *The Catcher in the Rye*, I teach *The Bell Jar* to showcase a young protagonist struggling with adulting (to grossly oversimplify both books), featuring Plath's gorgeous language and empathy. The writers I share in my class include Claudia Rankine, Eileen Myles, Leslie Jamison, Jamaica Kincaid, Natalie Diaz, Grace Paley, Ada Limón, Maggie Nelson, Morgan Parker, all authors I admire for not only their work on the page but the work they do in the world.

My first day of class was in January. It wasn't a beautiful

fall day, all ochre leaves and light sweaters; instead, it was freezing. Even though it was 2018, almost twenty years after my time in Mr. North's classroom, years into the widespread use of dry-erase boards, my heart dropped when I walked into the room: There was a chalkboard.

My classroom had no windows, there was no afternoon sun like in my high school, only fluorescent lamps buzzing softly. The walls were white, no posters, no bookshelves, no specificity. I had no traditional desk, just a larger plastic and metal table to spread my papers out in front of me. The classroom couldn't have been more different. But, still. I walked to the blackboard, picked up the same white chalk Mr. North had used in front of me almost daily, and wrote my own name for my fifteen students to read: PROFESSOR WOOD.

I had forgotten what chalk smelled like, somehow tactile, soft. The way it sounds when you write—the tap of it, the slow draw of lines and the squeak when your hand turns. I had forgotten what it feels like to take a piece of chalk in your hand. I blinked at my own writing. Had I ever even written on a blackboard before? I must have. But I could only see Mr. North's cursive, his words, his hand. I felt my mouth go wet and I swallowed. I held the chalk harder, and noticed my own sleeve was now kissed with white. I looked at the chalk again, in *my* hand now. I underlined my name, turned to my students, and began my first class.

———

From the very first semester, I saw her in my class: a girl who was young, gifted, and sad. Vulnerable. Every semester there is at least one student who is in a dark place in her life, who looks lost and alone. This is the student who emails me a lot, asking questions that I think she knows the answers to already but she's looking to connect. The student who comes early to class, stays late, walks out with me into the sunshine to talk about how much she loved the reading. This often happens when we read *The Bell Jar*. The first time I saw her, really saw her, it struck me: this is how I was. *That's me.*

This is not to disavow the agency, maturity, or intelligence of my students. Even the youngest ones, at eighteen, are (mostly) legal adults. Practically grown-ups. Some truly are, already, grown-ups. But still. They're also teenagers. Most have never lived alone, and still don't, living in dorms with roommates. Many have never paid rent, cooked a meal for themselves. They have not legally bought alcohol. Many do not have credit cards. They have never had a full-time job and bills. Now, at thirty-six, I feel like they are children. When I talk to the ones who stand out the most—the girls who are sad and talented and looking for help without ever actually saying that—I realize: when I blossomed under the attention and care of my teacher, I was asking for the support I desperately needed. I wasn't asking to be fucked.

After I had been teaching for a few semesters, I reread my high school journals. I had already begun writing about what had happened to me in classrooms in high school, hotel rooms after that. I had already begun to try to capture it on the page.

I read the notebooks carefully, searching for clues about

what really happened then, the facts of my situation. Most things in my memory from that time outside of the teacher are so hazy. Like looking through a mirror that's mottled and shaded. I try to touch my teenage self and it's only cold glass. Only moments with Mr. North are truly clear, sharp, concrete. Was it really love?

And then I found the entry for November 20 of my senior year. In it I detailed how that day, in his study hall, where I wasn't supposed to be but he gifted me with hall passes to make it okay, he asked me for my bra size. He pushed, offering to trade the size of his dick for the size of my breasts. *Are you scared?* Curious, and flattered, I didn't want to be a baby. The last thing I wanted was for him to not think I was the strong, powerful, sexy woman I was. So I took his offer. Later that afternoon I wrote in my journal, *Oh my god I can't stop blushing. Oh my god.* In that box of mementos I found three hall passes from that same day with his signature.

The entry wasn't a surprise. I remembered that happening. But in my mind, I thought it was much later—in May of my senior year, only weeks before I graduated and when I was already eighteen, when our physical relationship was within reach. But it wasn't. It was only weeks after we had first met, introduced by Ms. Croix, who most certainly thought she was helping me. I was seventeen. Mr. North was supposed to be helping me with my writing. I wanted to be a poet or write books when I grew up. I just wanted to improve my craft and feel like someone cared.

The faces of my students, my undergraduates, flashed inside me. I would never touch a student. I would never ask a

student for something like her bra size. I would never tell
her she's sexy. I would never ask her to keep a secret. I only
let them call me Professor Wood, never by my first name.
My emails and other written communications are always
kind, firm, and authoritative. No smiley faces. No exclamation points. *This is not a relationship, I am your teacher.* The few
times a male student has tried to flirt with me, I've shut it
down immediately, and become more formal with them, if
that is even possible.

Now that I had my own students, I became truly angry about what had happened to me. I understood just how
deeply, darkly inappropriate it would be to *ever, ever* cross a
line like that with one of them. I knew I would never dare
cross that line.

It was there, on that November 20 entry, so plain: Nothing I thought about what happened to me was true. Nothing
about what happened to me, or about *Lolita* at all, was about
love. Much less true love. I had known this, but reading it
in my own handwriting on lined paper was painful in a new
way. When I wrote those lines in my journal, I wasn't some
powerful, sexy grown-up. I was a child being manipulated,
being preyed upon. I was the victim of a predator. And I'm
sure I wasn't the only one.

I had heard by now that he had quit teaching, that he
left my high school only a few years later, his contract not
renewed because of rumors of another affair with an even
younger student. And I have been told about similar expe-
riences by dozens of women, even by my students, in workshops and at my M.F.A. and at readings and other places

where people heard I was writing this book. I learned how not special I am after all.

—

Every time I teach undergraduates, we read *Lolita* as the culmination to our semester. There's always a handful who have already read the book, but everyone knows what it's about. They say things like,

"A girl who needs attention."

"A pedophile."

"It's all an extended metaphor for the beauty of language."

"A creepy dude who takes advantage of a teenager."

None of them are wrong.

We only read the first ten chapters of the book—I now see *Lolita* clearly for what it is: beautiful, problematic, and too long, and so I never assign the novel in its entirety.

I hand out printouts of the first chapter, along with crayons, and we read the opening: *Lolita, light of my life, fire of my loins.* We read it aloud around the room, as many times as it takes so everyone says her name: *Lo. Li. Ta.* I have my students mark in crayon every time they notice a poetic device in use—alliteration, repetition, assonance, consonance, allusions. They notice there are lots of l's in the section, lots of t's. That her name is written eleven times in only four paragraphs. That the first and last word of the book is "Lolita." How all this adds up to telling the reader from the very first page that this is a book that is obsessed not only with seducing you, the reader, but with a girl named Lolita.

"This is really intense."

"Wait, that's not even her *actual* name."

"See? It's all about language."

"It's like putting flowers on a grave; it's beautiful but it doesn't hide what's awful about it."

Sometimes a jolt will run through my chest in the classroom, a flash of old hurt cut open. What my life could have been. And then I breathe and say inside a refrain, a spell of resilience I cast on myself as a reminder: Lolita *is dead. I survived. I survived.*

We look closely at certain chapters, then look at the Edgar Allan Poe poem "Annabel Lee." My students point out the lines where Nabokov apes Poe's language (*I was a child and she was a child . . . In a princedom by the sea*), showing how the use of allusions underpins Humbert's authority, how it makes him appear smarter and more powerful, even though they aren't really his words at all. How it's all a con. They buzz in our discussions—

"What the hell?"

"Can't he get his own fancy wordplay? Why does he have to appropriate other writers?"

"It's all a metaphor, you guys. . . ."

"Yeah, I don't get why people think this is so great. Half of this isn't even original."

Then we read the essay "Men Explain *Lolita* to Me" by Rebecca Solnit, bringing in the larger cultural context of the history of the abuse of young women in "classic" novels. We talk about how our culture defines "great writers"—who is deemed a genius, who is not—and the way those definitions all too often line up along gender lines.

The last piece we read aloud together in class is a new classic McSweeney's spoof, "If Women Wrote Men the Way Men Write Women." After more than three months together, everyone is in on the joke. We all laugh together, filling the classroom with happy noise.

I teach *Lolita* the way I wish it had been taught to me. I tell my students how some people still say it is a story about love, but I think differently. I don't tell them anything about my own experience; I would never be that personal with a student. I never want to blur a line. I stick to what's on the page.

—

When I teach *Lolita*, I bring in my own copy of the book. The one the teacher gave me surely is dissolved, re-created as mulch and dirt in that patch of woods in Ithaca. In my personal copy, I have notes written all over the margins, sentences underlined in pencil, sometimes just an exclamation point on the side of the page. Painstakingly, I try to find something new each time I read it, even if it's painful and unsettling. I always do. This past semester was no different. Yes, *Lolita* is beautiful. But yes, it's also terrible. We can hold both in our hands.

My most recent class was all young women. The subtitle of the course, "Powerful Women," creates a certain amount of self-selection. These have been my best students yet, even though I think that at the end of every semester. The women were smart, sharp, articulate, and insightful. They made connections I wish I had the ability to make when I was their age, they understood that the language is only the first part of the story. They understood. I didn't. The mixture of joy and sorrow this brings fills me to the brim.

In many ways, I still want to be like *Lolita*. To create something beautiful from something so terrible is my deepest desire. When I teach *Lolita*, I try to make my pain have a purpose, to impact my students in supportive, meaningful ways—in the ways I wish the book had impacted me. I can't change what happened to me. I try to do the little I can to make sure what happened to me doesn't happen again.

This past semester, on our last class, my students gave me chocolates and a card they all signed, thanking me for our time together. I pushed my lips together as I smiled, trying to keep my overfull heart from breaking through. I closed the book.

acknowledgments

Writing is a lonely art, but I was never alone in this.

None of this would have been possible without my agent, Rachel Vogel, who saw potential in me and my writing and always fought for me. I am so grateful for you over all these years.

This book bloomed under my editor, Sarah Murphy. Thank you for your unyielding belief in me and my book, especially in the moments when I had little of my own.

I can never thank the team who cared for this project at Flatiron Books enough, including Sydney Jeon, Lauren Bittrich, Claire McLaughlin, Katherine Turro, Matie Argiropoulos, and Keith Hayes. You treated this book as if it were something precious and worthwhile.

I have the unwavering support of my family, which I can never replace: my mom, dad, little sister, and my grandmother. They gave me permission to write and be a writer, again and again. I love you all.

Thank you to Ashely Lopez, my literary life partner and the very best friend, for never saying no—whether to a second set of eyes no matter how late at night, getting a much needed drink, or giving me the truest feedback. Or even to starting a literary journal. You were there every step of the way, and I cannot wait to repay you in the future.

Christie Spillane, who always knew I could do more and supported me in this journey for more than fifteen years through countless phone calls, visits, cat pictures, and love. It finally happened!

The biggest thank you to my fellow teacher and classmate Michele Filgate, who is always there for me and my writing, and whose generosity is legendary. You are a true friend.

Debra Hanusick Gerstner gave me the much needed push out of my comfortable suburban nest to try writing *for real* in NYC. I will never forget that moment in your kitchen, Deb, when you told me I should do this even though I was so scared. You knew I wouldn't fail. Thank you.

I am so grateful to have the friendship, kindness, and enthusiasm of David Merrell in my life. I knew when we met that first day in class that we would be friends. I'm so glad I was right.

This book would only be a shell of itself without the time, attention, and care of Darin Strauss, Melissa Febos, Nick Flynn, Laura Sims, Lynn Steger Strong, Mitchell Jackson, Katie Kitamura, and Paul Lisicky. I can only hope to make you proud.

I was lucky enough to have many of my writer-heroes in my corner from the beginning. Your guidance, support, and brilliance were everything in this process. Thank you to Hannah Tinti, Zadie Smith, Susan Choi, Garrard Conley, Joanna Yas, Rachel Lyon, Rob Spillman, Piper Weiss, John Freeman, and Alexander Chee, for always answering my many questions and cheering me on.

The process of finishing a book would have been terrifying without T Kira Madden, whose texts, hugs, and support made it ok. Your honesty and vulnerability were limitless, and I deeply love and appreciate you.

Raven Leilani was a shining star traveling right beside me through the journey of publication, and I had the gift of always being able to look to you for in-the-moment insight, friendship, and the space to be real. I love you, my book-birthday twin!

I cannot be more grateful for my *Pigeon Pages* flock of wonderful, wild women and folx who always bring joy, love, and expertise to our literary journal and readings. I started *Pigeon Pages* because I was afraid I would end up a lonely writer, lost. With such a glorious group, I am certain that won't be true for any of us.

I could not ask for better friends and first readers. You are the reason this book happened. Thank you, thank you, thank you to Jessica Williams, Kyle Dillon Hertz, Natassja Schiel, Anna Godbersen, Adam Dalva, Claire Werkiser, Lindsey Comstack, Bernard Ferguson, Katie Martin, Marisa Seigel, Emily Brout, Peach Neeley, Lilly Dancyger, Chris Veteri, Jason Gallen, Melissa Wacks, Madeleine Mori, Jiordan Castle, Hannah Bae, Nadra Mabrouk, and Rachel Barton.

While this book is about a terrible teacher, I have been

lucky enough to also have some wonderful, deeply impactful teachers, including Leigh Stein, Paul Cody, Jason Ockert, Andre Dubus III, Jericho Brown, Harryette Mullen, April Krassner, Ruth Danon, Chris Piegaro, Gigi Marks, Sherry Mason, and Mary Donnelly. You showed me the power of teaching, and how it can be used for good.

Thank you to all of my students, the ones who I have already had and the ones who I haven't met yet. I only hope to be the kind of teacher I needed and deserved. You are who I show up for, on the page and in the classroom.

As a writer, I have found community and financial support in many places, including New York University as a Dean's Fellow and Goldwater Fellow; as a summer resident at Paragraph; Tin House Workshop; Catapult; Poets House; Westport Writers' Workshop; the Author's Guild; and *Epiphany* magazine. This was vital for me, and kept me going.

It might seem silly to thank my cats, but it is true. Thank you to Ginger Rogers, Nora Charles, Rita Hayworth, Elizabeth Taylor, and Grace Kelly for never leaving my side and always listening over the past fifteen years.

And thank you, to you, dear reader. I never thought anyone would care about what happened to me, and to others, and what still happens. Thank you for reading this.